P9-DGR-186

"Entrepreneurs are delivering unprecedented customer value by harnessing innovative business models to provide top-quality custom products at affordable prices. *Custom Nation* takes a good look at the history of customization, who's doing it well, and where it is headed."

—*Robert Keane, CEO and Founder of Vistaprint*

"As CEO of a company whose products are driven by customization, I can confidently say that consumers want specialized, ownable products—and this book shows you how to build a loyal customer base and improve your bottom line."

—*Jeffrey Housenbold, President and CEO of Shutterfly*

"Anthony Flynn applied customization to turn the humble nutrition bar into a personalized experience. In *Custom Nation*, he shares his insight on how to profit from the fact that all people are different. A must-read for all entrepreneurs—and anyone else interested in the future of business."

—*Frank Piller, Head of MIT's Smart Customization Group*

"*Custom Nation* identifies a new space for an entrepreneur to create and grow a business, marrying the evolving technologies of customized production and distribution with the enabling power of internet communications to closely fit customer needs. It gives a newcomer concrete guidance for initiating and establishing a solid platform for future growth. 'What do I do on Monday?' is a focus question for the handbook section of the book, and the book will tell you in clear and usable terms."

—*Norman E. Toy, Columbia Business School Adjunct Professor of Finance & Economics*

"*Custom Nation* is an engaging and insightful look at the evolution of customization and how individual consumers are now the driving force in the future of retail. Flynn and Vencat have created an insightful how-to guide for anyone looking to start their own customization business based on expert sources and their own customization entrepreneurial experience. A quick and entertaining read, *Custom Nation* captures the essence of how and why customization has become such a crucial part of the modern consumer experience. The book makes it easy for aspiring customizers to leverage this wealth of knowledge to build the successful CIY business of their dreams."

—Jeff Beaver, Co-Founder and Chief Product Officer of Zazzle

"Customization is the buzzword in business these days and *Custom Nation* explains how to approach customizing effectively and make the most out of it."

—Jan-Christoph Goetze, CEO and Founder of PersonalNOVEL

"Emily Flynn Vencat and Anthony Flynn have brought the future to you today. This book chronicles how humankind's drive for self-expression has evolved and where it is heading."

—Bob Marino, CEO of CafePress

CUSTOM NATION

HF
5415.125
.F59
2012

CUSTOM NATION

WHY CUSTOMIZATION IS THE FUTURE OF BUSINESS AND HOW TO PROFIT FROM IT

ANTHONY FLYNN

EMILY FLYNN VENCAT

with Dennis Flynn

BenBella

BenBella Books, Inc.
Dallas, Texas

KVCC KALAMAZOO VALLEY
COMMUNITY COLLEGE
LIBRARY

All rights reserved. No part of this book may be used or reproduced in any manner whatsoever without written permission except in the case of brief quotations embodied in critical articles or reviews.

Copyright © 2012 by Anthony Flynn and Emily Flynn Vencat

Shutterfly and CafePress images used with permission.

BENBELLA

BenBella Books, Inc.
10300 N. Central Expressway, Suite 400
Dallas, TX 75231
www.benbellabooks.com
Send feedback to feedback@benbellabooks.com

Printed in the United States of America
10 9 8 7 6 5 4 3 2 1

Library of Congress Cataloging-in-Publication Data is available for this title.
978-1-937856-10-6

Editing by Debbie Harmsen
Copyediting by Lisa Miller
Proofreading by James Fraleigh and Brittany Dowdle
Indexing by WordCo Indexing Services, Inc.
Cover design by Kit Sweeney
Text design and composition by Cape Cod Compositors, Inc.
Printed by Bang Printing

Distributed by Perseus Distribution
(www.perseusdistribution.com)

To place orders through Perseus Distribution:
Tel: (800) 343-4499
Fax: (800) 351-5073
E-mail: orderentry@perseusbooks.com

Significant discounts for bulk sales are available. Please contact Glenn Yeffeth at glenn@benbellabooks.com or (214) 750-3628.

Dedicated to

K
E
A V A
I
N

CUSTOM
NATION

Contents

section 1

AMERICA AS A CUSTOM NATION

CHAPTER 1

The 21st Century's Custom Revolution

I woke up to the sound of my BlackBerry vibrating. I grabbed it and glanced at my emails—there were thousands pouring in. Suddenly, my phone rang. It was PayPal, the payment processor. "Do you have a minute?" the voice said. "Yes," I replied. Then the PayPal employee said something like, "You've had such a large amount of money come into your account in the last week, we believe you could be involved in illegal activity. What business are you in?"

I was floored. "I sell energy bars," I said. I could tell the PayPal employee wasn't convinced that I was telling the truth. And he was right to be dubious. Really, that's only half the story.

What he didn't realize was that during the week before that call, all the hard work I had put into launching a revolutionary new business had suddenly paid off. Those thousands of emails pouring in were customer orders. I'm Anthony Flynn, the owner of YouBar, and during that single week in February 2008, my nutrition bar business had been featured in *The New York Times*, DailyCandy, National Public Radio's *Marketplace*, ABC, NBC and Fox—with headlines like: "With These Nutrition Bars, Every Order Is Special," "Let Your Taste Buds and Imagination Take Over" and "A Nutrition Bar Created by You, for You."

Those headlines held the clue to what I hadn't told PayPal yet. I'm not just in the business of selling energy bars. My secret is that my company sells completely *customized* energy bars. We make all of our bars to meet the exact ingredient, taste and nutritional needs of each of our individual clients, and we sell them for roughly the same price as the existing high-quality bars on the market.

My business revolutionized the world of nutrition bars, but we are actually just one small example of the massive upheaval in manufacturing that is happening right now. As we get deeper into the 2010s, the most successful companies in every industry in the United States—from food to fashion—are ditching mass production in favor of customization. This shift is so enormous and all-encompassing that it ultimately promises to define the coming decades as powerfully as the Industrial Revolution defined the 19th and 20th centuries. It is 2012, and we are at the beginning of the 21st century's Custom Revolution.

The 21st Century's Industrial Revolution

Just look around and you'll see the Custom Revolution catching fire everywhere: Nike's custom sneakers, Burberry's custom trench coats, Levi's custom jeans, Dell's custom computers, Mattel's custom Barbie Dolls, Hallmark's custom storybooks, Mars' custom M&M's, Ford's custom Mustangs, Pottery Barn's custom furniture and—of course—Starbucks' custom coffees.

Even the nonmaterialistic parts of our lives are teeming with customized purchases. Netflix plays personalized programming. Pandora broadcasts tailored-to-you radio stations. eHarmony offers personalized love matches. Google flashes just-for-you advertising sidebars. Facebook delivers customized newsfeeds. Amazon makes entertainment recommendations especially for you. And there are iPhone apps that sync with

Google Maps to tell you which delicious nearby restaurant to hit after the movie your other iPhone app recommended.

America is becoming a nation of customizers. And the one new rule for successful businesses across the country is simple: Customize for your clients. What PayPal saw that day in February wasn't drug dealing or money laundering—it was the new Custom Revolution in action. Customization is completely changing the way we do business, and this book holds the reasons behind this enormous shift and the unwritten (until now) lessons for how to do it right.

America is becoming a nation of customizers. And the one new rule for successful businesses across the country is simple: Customize for your clients.

■ No Longer a Bad Business Model

In the 20th century, conventional wisdom was that customization was a bad business model for anything except a small niche seller because it was expensive and slow. But that was so last century. Today, forget everything you thought you knew about customizing. A jaw-dropping number of Fortune 500 companies now offer some sort of customized product or feature customization as a key part of their marketing strategies. In addition to the names mentioned earlier, this customizing-company list includes Procter & Gamble, PepsiCo, Chrysler, Coca-Cola, The Walt Disney Co., General Motors, Harley-Davidson, HP, The Boeing Co., Home Depot, Johnson & Johnson and Bed Bath & Beyond. In 2010 alone, the sportswear giant Nike sold more than $100 million worth of *totally customized*, *made-to-order* sneakers (and, incidentally, today *every* single big athletic shoe company in the world—from Reebok to Adidas—has stepped up to offer custom shoes). Meanwhile, dozens of fashion-forward shoe companies, like selve and Shoes of Prey, march down the runway with everything from choose-your-own-heel-height custom stilettos to design-it-yourself ballet flats.

It's not just the big incumbents that are creating the Custom Revolution. Companies with completely custom business models are popping up everywhere and breaking what used to be thought of as a glass ceiling for customizers: the billion-dollar mark.

Before the early 2000s, there was only one retail company with a truly custom business model that had broken this barrier—Dell Inc. In 1985, Michael Dell started making built-to-order computers from his dorm room. Today Dell Inc. is worth a whopping $27 billion. Even so, in its infant years many believed the company's success was a one-off anomaly because early attempts to copy the model failed.

No more. Thanks to massive technological innovations, care of the internet and the digitization of information, the custom business model is now verging on the billion-dollar mark all over the place. Vistaprint, a printing company that specializes in making custom goods for small businesses, boasts a market cap of $1.3 billion. Shutterfly, a company that makes customized photo gifts, is worth approximately $1 billion. Pandora, the custom radio provider, is worth $1.6 billion.

And right behind these colossal customizers are dozens of customizing companies that are well on their way to a billion. Blue Nile, a diamond jeweler that allows customers to design their own rings and earrings, is worth $550 million. CafePress, a company that makes custom goods of all shapes and sizes—from flip-flops to wall art—launched a successful initial public offering (IPO) in March 2012 that valued the company at more than $288 million.[1] Zazzle, a company that customizes everything from T-shirts to skateboards, pulled in more than $100 million in revenue in 2011, with profits in the eight-digit range and as many as 24 million visitors per month.

As a nutrition bar company, we at YouBar are, of course, smaller than these heavy hitters, but our annual revenues are well into seven figures, our website clocks more than half a million visits a year, and we've proudly produced millions of totally customized bars in just six years in business.

■ The New Business Rules in the Age ■ of Customization

Customization is so ubiquitous as the new business model that there's a scramble at the world's top companies and research universities to codify the lessons of how to do business in this brand-new era. Since that February when I got the call from PayPal, I've been invited to give lectures on customization at universities like the University of Southern California (USC), the University of California, Berkeley and UCLA; I've been interviewed in major business media, like National Public Radio's *Marketplace* and Fox; and I've been asked to consult to large companies that are adding customization to their current mass-produced offerings.

What they all want to know is, *How do you make customization work on a grand scale?*

Whenever a new way to do business takes over, there are always new rules to follow. But, since the Custom Revolution is just now happening, those rules haven't yet been written down, and the case study lessons from companies doing it right haven't yet been put together—until now. This book shows how businesses are making customization work and how you can follow suit.

For would-be entrepreneurs, the custom business model is the new gold rush. With customization, you don't have to have the funding of a Fortune 500 behind you to make it to seven-digit sales; all you need is a good idea and customization. In the following pages, I'll tell you about dozens of smart entrepreneurs, like Jan-Christoph Goetze of Personal-NOVEL and Max Wittrock of mymuesli, who launched enormously successful businesses based on customization with as little as $5,000 in seed funding.

I will outline in this book exactly how you, too, can use customization to launch a successful new business, or exponentially increase sales in your existing business. I'll show you how, with customization, you can differentiate your product from your competitors', generate phenomenal press and—of course—get that call from PayPal.

■The Genesis of This Book

The knowledge laid out in this book doesn't just come from personal experience. To get customization right, it is vital to learn from the best. So when I decided I wanted to write a book to share the wisdom of customization, I knew I needed someone who was experienced at interviewing top executives, could tell the story of customization's rise and, most of all, was a great writer.

The answer of who I needed was obvious even before I asked it. My sister, Emily Flynn Vencat, is a business journalist. Emily's first job out of college was at *Newsweek*'s London bureau, where she ultimately became the magazine's London-based business writer. She has also worked on staff for The Associated Press and written stories that have been published in the *International Herald Tribune*, the *Columbia Journalism Review* and *USA Today*. Emily has interviewed some of the biggest names in the business world, including Virgin boss Richard Branson, Carlyle Group cofounder David Rubenstein and the late Body Shop founder, Anita Roddick. I knew my sister would make the perfect coauthor.

However, persuading Emily to write this book with me wasn't easy. When I first brought the idea up to her, she was skeptical. "Customization is an interesting trend," she said, "but I don't think it's book-worthy." My response caught her attention. "Customization isn't just a trend," I said. "It's the new way Americans are going to do business. It's the new mass production. By the year 2040, everything we consume—food, clothing, cars, advertisements, trips abroad—will be customized to meet our exact desires. *Everything.* I'm willing to put money on it."

Customization isn't just a trend.... It's the new way Americans are going to do business. It's the new mass production. By the year 2040, everything we consume—food, clothing, cars, advertisements, trips abroad—will be customized to meet our exact desires. *Everything.* I'm willing to put money on it.

Emily was willing to take my bet. She left my Hollywood apartment still shaking her head, but a few hours later, I got a call from her. Emily told me that on her way home she had driven past Los Angeles' famous (and notoriously trend-setting) Hollywood and Vine intersection. Within blocks of Hollywood and Vine, she passed a Bed Bath & Beyond advertising personalized shower curtains and doormats, a *New York Times* ad broadcasting custom homepages for subscribers, an HSBC flyer for customized banking, a Victoria's Secret window advertising bras that feel "custom made," and The Counter, a new burger chain whose slogan is "Custom Built Burgers."

"I've driven through that neighborhood a million times," Emily said. "It used to be all McDonald's Big Macs, Blockbuster videos and Louis Vuitton bags. But that simply isn't the case anymore. Customization—even the word itself—is literally all over the place. I'm in."

Most of what you'll read in this book you can't find anywhere else. Emily and I are extremely grateful to the visionary entrepreneurs and insightful academics whose candid interviews and generosity of advice made this book possible, including (but not at all limited to) Robert Keane of Vistaprint, Bob Marino of CafePress, Bobby Beaver and Jeff Beaver of Zazzle, Jeffrey Housenbold of Shutterfly, Dan Ariely of Duke University and Frank Piller of the Massachusetts Institute of Technology (MIT). In the following pages, Emily and I will draw from the experiences of these thinkers and business people and many other inspirational entrepreneurs to show you how you too can launch a successful new custom business or add a component of customization to your existing business. The secret of a successful 21st century business? Customization. And the secret to doing that right? Read on.

CHAPTER 2

The End of Mass Production
How America Became
a Custom Nation

In the years between 1950 and 2000, Americans embraced an enormous shift in our age-old habits. In eating, we went from home-cooked to fast food. In clothing, we went from home-sewn to mass-produced. In entertainment, we went from home storytelling to blockbuster TV shows. In short, our entire lives went from unique and one-of-a-kind to mass-produced and dime-a-dozen. During the epitome of these years, the 1960s and 1970s, we all watched the same TV shows (*Gunsmoke*, *The Andy Griffith Show*), ate the same foods (regular Cokes, Big Macs) and drove the same cars (VW Beetles, wide Cadillacs).

Now, at the beginning of the 21st century, we're moving into the next major shift in consumption: from mass-produced to totally customized. This seismic movement toward custom everything is, in many ways, the pendulum swinging back to the way we used to live. By moving from pre-made to made-to-order, we're eating fresher and less-processed food, we're living with goods (furniture, cars, homes) that are customized to our needs and styles and we're wearing clothes that fit our styles and bodies perfectly because they were made for us.

However, even though there are echoes of an earlier idyll, there are significant ways in which the burgeoning custom revolution is brand-new.

Before the Industrial Revolution, customization was the norm because we did everything ourselves, like cooking stews and sewing curtains. But today's customization isn't Do-It-Yourself (DIY); it's Create-It-Yourself, or what I like to call CIY. Create-It-Yourself is when you get to do all the fun parts related to making something new, like designing the flames emblazoned on the side of your Mustang or choosing the exact ingredients in your gluten-free nutrition bars, without having to do the hard work of stencil painting or wheatless cooking yourself.

Before the turn of the millennium, CIY was the preserve of the ultra-wealthy. It was only the elite who could brag about having customized clothing and food from the likes of Savile Row tailors and live-in personal chefs. But since the turn of the 21st century, CIY on an industrial scale (what's known in academic circles as "mass customization") has finally become possible. Thanks to game-changing technological innovations—like the internet's ability to connect producers directly to consumers without the heavy markups of middlemen retailers, and the development of relatively inexpensive online configurators that allow consumers to design their own products easily from home computers—CIY goods are now almost as affordable as mass-produced ones.

There are few business minds that know as much about America's current evolution from mass production to CIY customization as Bob Marino. As the CEO of CafePress, Bob took the custom-everything company public in March 2012. The successful IPO earned gross proceeds of $80 million and valued the company at more than $250 million. Bob told me why he thinks mass production is soon going to be history:

> The Industrial Revolution changed consumer behavior by giving everyone the same factory-made stuff. This took away a lot of consumers' individuality, but it made people happy by giving them access to a much greater number of goods than they were previously accustomed to getting. And so that was how Americans consumed goods during the 20th century. Now, at the beginning of the 21st century, we've reached the next frontier. Now goods are commonplace. So the question is: How can we make them *uncommon*? And the answer to that question is customization. It's the single strongest driving force in how to please your customers today. Customization is the new Industrial Revolution.

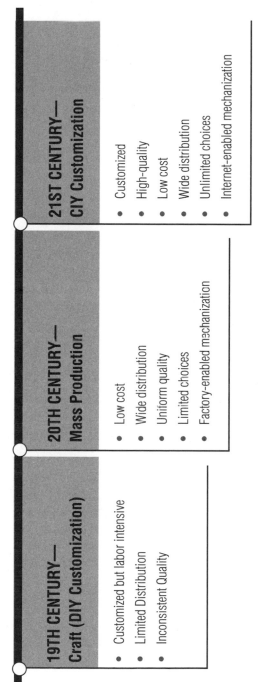

19TH CENTURY—
Craft (DIY Customization)

- Customized but labor intensive
- Limited Distribution
- Inconsistent Quality

20TH CENTURY—
Mass Production

- Low cost
- Wide distribution
- Uniform quality
- Limited choices
- Factory-enabled mechanization

21ST CENTURY—
CIY Customization

- Customized
- High-quality
- Low cost
- Wide distribution
- Unlimited choices
- Internet-enabled mechanization

Figure 2.1 HISTORY OF AMERICAN MANUFACTURING

■The 20th Century: Have It All

With goods being—as Bob puts it—so "common" now, it can be difficult to remember just how recently our choices of goods of all sorts were incredibly limited. One of the most concrete examples of the boom in available goods can be seen in the aisles of America's food stores. When my grandfather Lester, who turned 92 in 2012, was growing up in Chicago in the 1920s, he helped his Russian immigrant parents run a fruit-and-vegetable store. Mass production of food products hadn't yet started en masse, and he remembers that the whole stock they carried then was what we'd now consider basic staples: tomatoes, potatoes, cucumbers, etc. There were no prepackaged foods, no crates of plastic drink bottles and no out-of-season watermelons. "I used to love when the watermelons arrived," he recalls vividly. "I'd eat so many!"

Indeed, during my grandfather's childhood, the average corner grocery store carried around 700 items. But, while everyone used these same staples to make everything they ate, people ate different foods than their neighbors because meals were cooked at home by their moms. Meals were hard work to make, and they were individualized.

Then mass production hit the food industry (just like it hit every industry). By the time my grandfather was raising his children in 1960, supermarkets had started stocking one-size-fits-all, ready-made meals that had been mass-produced in factories, and fast-food restaurants were providing similarly one-food-fits-all products on every busy street corner. Thanks to these mass-produced convenience foods, like Idahoan instant mashed potatoes and Swanson frozen TV dinners, the number of unique items that my grandfather could find at his local store exploded nearly ten-fold to 6,000. But while choice grew, the diets of Americans actually shrank to be more similar than ever before. We ate the same TV dinners, whether your family heritage was Polish, Indian, Chinese or Irish.

By the mid-1970s, mass production had effectively given everyone access to the same—well—everything, and goods were utterly commonplace. With this being the case, people stopped seeing simply "having" as being enviable, and once again started craving things tailored especially for them.

So mass production went into overdrive to offer as many versions of their products as possible and to appeal to every single type of person. The year my grandfather's first grandchild was born in 1980, the number of unique items he could find at his local market had jumped from the 6,000 that was standard in 1960 to 14,000. And today, soon after the birth of his first great-grandchild, that number has more than tripled again to 48,000.[1] In other words, in my grandfather's lifetime, the amount of goods he can find at his local store has gone from 700 to 48,000.

In my grandfather's lifetime, the amount of choices he can find at his local store has gone from 700 to 48,000.

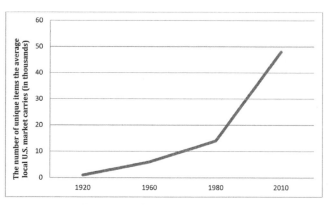

Figure 2.2   SUPERMARKET CHOICE

In some ways, Coca-Cola is the most obvious example of our recent growing thirst for abundant choice. There are more than 20 types of Coca-Cola on the market today, including Coca-Cola Zero, Coca-Cola Cherry and Diet Coke with Lime. But for nearly a *century*—from when the soda first launched in 1886 all the way until 1982—there was just one: regular Coke. Likewise, PepsiCo's Tropicana brand now sells 20 varieties of pulped juice, up from just six as recently as 2004.[2]

■The Long Tail

The most outstanding economic explanation of this phenomenon (choice everywhere!) was laid out by Chris Anderson in his 2006 *New York Times* bestseller *The Long Tail: Why the Future of Business Is Selling Less of More*. In it Anderson explains that, thanks to modern efficiencies in distribution, manufacturing and marketing, it's now profitable to make lots of different products to appeal to lots of different small niches, instead of a single big-run item for the masses.

As his prime examples, Anderson cites the entertainment industry. With the arrival of "shelf" space—unlimited and geographically transcendent internet storefronts—the new purveyors of media, like Netflix (for movies) and Amazon (for books), don't make all their money from a handful of megahits. That was the business model of late-20th century Goliaths—like Blockbuster and Borders. (Blockbuster filed for bankruptcy protection in 2010; Borders filed in 2011 and closed its doors for good later that year.)

Rather, the new leaders make high percentages of their income from the tiny sales of lots and lots of different niche bands and old cult movies. As people increasingly watch and listen to exactly what they want, exactly when they want to and exactly where they want to (such as on their smartphones), we're no longer tied to a handful of hits. Indeed, Anderson points out: "As much as the blockbuster era seems like the natural state of things, it is, as we've seen, mostly an artifact of late-20th century broadcast technologies. Before then most culture was local; in the future it will be affinity-based."[3]

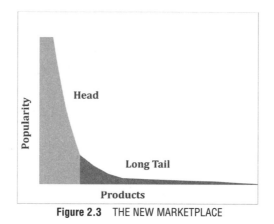

Figure 2.3 THE NEW MARKETPLACE

But our new way of consuming goods doesn't stop with small "affinity-based" niches, like the indie garage band with a handful of devo tees or Diet Cherry Coke. It gets even smaller.

■ Niches of One: The Early 21st Century ■ Transition to Customization

The latest trend is for companies to offer goods made for the smallest niche market possible: one person. The first signs of this transition to mass customization can be seen as far back as the mid-1970s. And, perhaps surprisingly, it hit the fast-food industry first. In 1976, Burger King had the then-revolutionary idea to differentiate itself from the likes of McDonald's and Wendy's by offering something then unheard of: burgers made-to-order with the toppings customers wanted. That year, the company launched its now-famous "Have It Your Way" campaign with a national TV commercial touting the fact that at Burger King you could get what you wanted on your burger. The commercial showed a woman ordering something that would now be considered almost ridiculously mundane—"extra ketchup"—while a voiceover explained: "You want your Whopper some special way, you'll get it!"[4]

Starting with Burger King, many of the early pioneers in customization were in the quick-service food and drink industries. In 1974, right around the same time that Burger King launched "Have It Your Way," Subway opened its first franchise restaurant in Connecticut. This set the scene for Subway—the first restaurant chain to make customization a central selling point—to explode from just 16 restaurants in 1974 to its current 36,000 global locations, which makes it the most ubiquitous chain restaurant in the world, boasting even more locations than McDonald's.[5]

Undeniably, the most culturally transformative example of customization came with Starbucks, which opened its first espresso bar in 1984. (The company dates back to 1971, but it only sold coffee beans—not coffee itself—for the first 13 years.) Thanks in large part to Starbucks, we're all so accustomed to customization that we don't think twice about ordering a "grande decaf three-pump vanilla soy latte," even though that drink is nowhere on the menu. In fact, in the Starbucks era, the static menu hanging behind the espresso machines at most coffee shops seems more decorative than informative—retro even.

Today, nearly all the big restaurants in every category, from Mexican food to frozen yogurt, make catering to their customers' individual tastes a key part of their strategies, whether it is the choose-your-own-ingredients Chipotle or the self-serve Yogurtland. Jamba Juice (opened in 1990) shot to prominence by letting customers design their own fresh juice drinks counter-side, instead of having to settle for a limited selection of pre-made combos. Chipotle (founded in 1993) sells custom burritos, Freshii (opened in 2005) sells custom salads and The Counter (opened in 2003) sells burgers that are so customizable that the company's tagline is "Custom Built Burgers." Yogurtland (opened in 2006) sells customizable frozen yogurt and has spawned dozens of imitators. "The number of restaurant orders that come in with customized elements these days is staggering," said

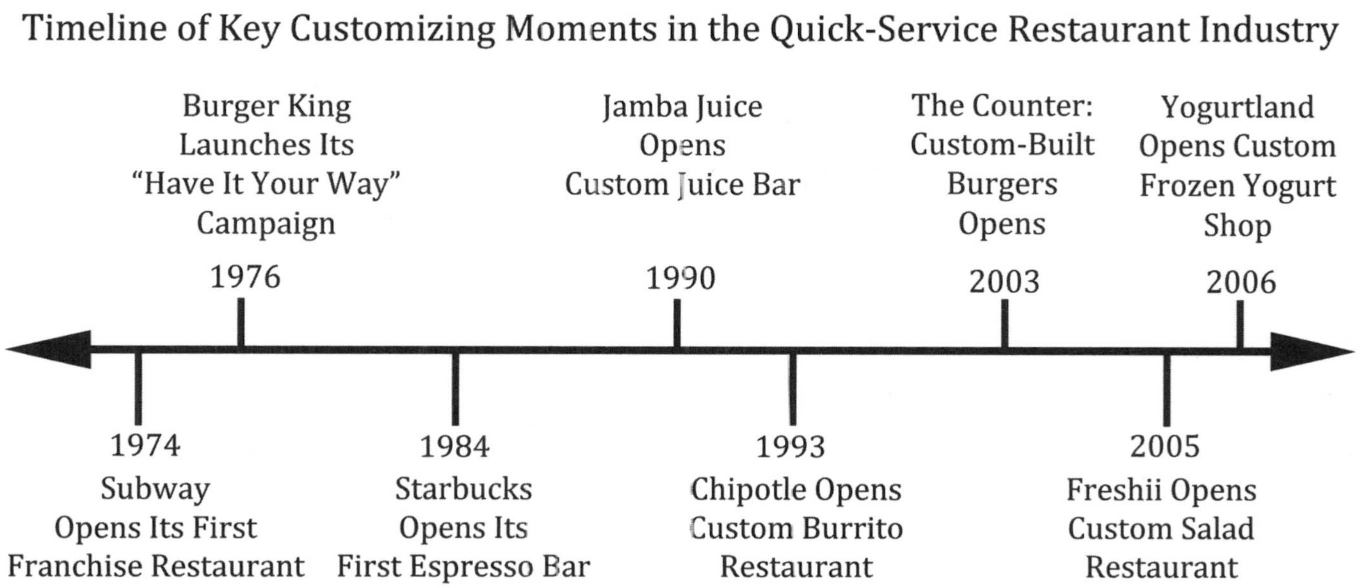

Timeline of Key Customizing Moments in the Quick-Service Restaurant Industry

1974 — Subway Opens Its First Franchise Restaurant

1976 — Burger King Launches Its "Have It Your Way" Campaign

1984 — Starbucks Opens Its First Espresso Bar

1990 — Jamba Juice Opens Custom Juice Bar

1993 — Chipotle Opens Custom Burrito Restaurant

2003 — The Counter: Custom-Built Burgers Opens

2005 — Freshii Opens Custom Salad Restaurant

2006 — Yogurtland Opens Custom Frozen Yogurt Shop

Figure 2.4 THE FAST-FOOD PIONEERS

19

Steven Goldstein, a partner at The Culinary Edge, a restaurant consultancy group. He estimated that around 25 percent of all restaurant orders are personalized by customers.

"The number of restaurant orders that come in with customized elements these days is staggering," said Steven Goldstein, a partner at The Culinary Edge, a restaurant consultancy group. He estimated that around 25 percent of all restaurant orders are personalized by customers.

■ Other Industries Start Going Custom

Customization as the norm couldn't come for other industries—like fashion, manufactured foods and automobiles—back in the 1970s, '80s or even '90s because during the 20th century, goods of those sorts were produced at factories and then sold at separate retail stores. By and large, producers had no direct contact with consumers (except through retailers) and so customization was impossible. At restaurants, on the other hand, the staff could give customers options, and customers could then order what they wanted fresh from the kitchen. But at clothing stores, for example, there were no tailors and seamstresses available to take custom orders, except at very expensive elite stores. And short of having a highly educated, highly paid expert (tailor, architect, jeweler, etc.) standing right beside them, consumers didn't have the tools to design exactly what they wanted. Imagine, for example, trying to sketch your perfect suit or dress. For the vast majority of us, our basic drawing skills and lack of knowledge about how materials work would make this utterly impossible.

The internet changed everything. With the widespread adoption of the internet in 2001 (the first year that more than 50 percent of Americans reported using it[6]), suddenly the technology was available for the producers of consumer goods to *customize affordably*. Consumers can now go to online stores and design their own products *without expert help*. At online stores like Indochino (for men's suits) and DressByDesign (for women's dresses), consumers take their measurements at home and then use fun, interactive online design tools to design their very own suits and dresses, which the companies then make to order.

This shift holds true for manufactured food products as well. At YouBar, for example, there is no way that consumers could have designed their own healthy energy bars effectively without a nutritionist beside them in the pre-internet age. Our website, which was created by a brilliant Web designer Garett Wenig allows consumers to change ingredients and see updates of their bars' nutrition facts (amount of fat, calories, etc.) in real time on a "nutrition calculator" as they choose from more than 100 different ingredient options.

Removing the need for on-hand expert help slashed a huge cost for customizers, but making custom products to order still costs more than mass production. Customizers get around this with their direct-to-consumer internet sales model. When producers sell directly to consumers, they eliminate retailers' typical markups of between 25 percent (in supermarkets) and 50 percent (in department stores), so even when production costs are 25 to 50 percent higher, the end price of the product is still the same.[7]

STRAIGHT TO THE PRODUCTION FLOOR

Robert Keane, the CEO and founder of Vistaprint, the $1.2 billion global printing firm, explained why affordable, large-scale customization simply couldn't happen before the internet's "digitization of information":

> In the past, it was very costly for companies to operate customizing business models because transferring information was expensive. Traditionally, for a customer to describe what they wanted, they would have to sit down with a highly paid designer, the designer would draw it up, and then the customer would have to sign off on a proof.

CONTINUES

CONTINUED

The digitization of everything in our lives allows information to be exchanged infinitely less expensively. If a customer wanted to change a business card design in the past, for example, that was costly. The designer would have to fix it personally, and then go back to the customer again for a sign-off. But now, the marginal economic cost of changes is nothing because the customer is able to do all that themselves just by using our software. The broad shift to digital everything allows that transfer of information. Customers' designs go straight to the production floor.

■ Levi's Proves It

The most famous case study proving that widespread affordable customization simply couldn't work before the internet comes from the world-famous jean maker Levi Strauss & Co. In 1994 Levi's began selling customized jeans, which it called "Personal Pair" and, later, "Original Spin." Consumers could walk into select stores around the country and have their measurements and style preferences taken by staff in computer-equipped dressing rooms. Staff would send the details via computer to a U.S.-based Levi Strauss factory, and several weeks later, the customer would receive a pair of custom jeans made just for them.

At first, Levi's Original Spin seemed like a huge success—a breakthrough! Customers loved them, the press wrote more than 1,000 articles about them and they even got included in manufacturing textbooks as an excellent early example of "mass customization" by a big-name corporation. But then, with very little fanfare, Levi's shut down Original Spin in 2003.

What went wrong? Customization was supposed to be the new way to buy jeans. Levi's was supposed to be *the* stellar example of mass customization gone mainstream. But there was a crucial problem: Original Spin never reached that many consumers. The custom jeans were only sold in select stores because they were labor-intensive to sell—trained staff had to take down all the consumers' preferences individually. This is a task that new internet design tools make completely *automatic*.

Sure enough, in 2010, Levi's launched a brand-new custom jean business, Curve ID. And, crucially, the new business is online and also in Levi's outlets. It offers women shopping on the internet (or in some stores) the enticing option to "Get a custom fitting in a few easy steps!" Curve ID isn't just turning everyday jeans into custom jeans; it's also turning a serious profit. In the third quarter of 2011, Levi's saw its revenue jump by 9 percent—a rise the company credited in large part to the success of Curve ID.

Several other large companies also failed in their first attempts at customization because they, too, tried too early—before consumers were comfortable using internet design tools and making purchases online. Among these too-early-to-catch-the-worm online businesses were General Mills' MyCereal (custom cereal) and Procter & Gamble's PersonalBlends (custom coffee). Both launched between 2000 and 2002, and neither survived for longer than 18 months. Their ideas were great, but they were just too early. In fact, today there are more than 10 companies selling custom coffee, and more than 15 companies offering customized cereal, including mymuesli, which had pulled in well over $1 million by 2008, just a year after launching.

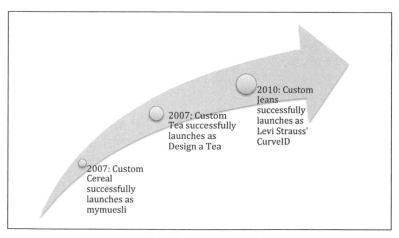

Figure 2.5 CUSTOM PROGRESSION

CEREAL ENTREPRENEURS

Cereal giant General Mills failed when it launched its custom cereal line in 2000. But seven years later, German startup my-muesli made a killing with the same idea. What did mymuesli do so right?

In 2006, three 20-something German buddies—Max Wittrock, Philipp Kraiss and Hubertus Bessau—didn't have jobs when they graduated from college. So they decided to start their own company. They had seen how the internet was making customization possible on a whole new level and decided to see how the concept would work with one of Germany's favorite breakfast foods: muesli.

With just a germ of an idea, very low rent costs and a lot of excitement, the three friends launched mymuesli.com in April 2007. The website offered German consumers the ability to design their own breakfast cereals—mixing and matching all sorts of oats, nuts, dried fruit and flakes—and then the company would make the cereal, put it in cool tubular boxes and send them to consumers' doorsteps.

They lived hand to mouth for the first few months, but they were certain their high-quality product would land on many a breakfast table as soon as word of mouth spread. Then, as luck would have it, the media caught on to them. With their innovative product, the photogenic trio took Germany by storm, landing glowing reviews in newspapers, magazines and television, and even winning the coveted "Startup of the Year" title in 2007 from Germany's Deutsche Startups. The founders still privately own the company, so its financial data is not publicly available. But Max told me that within the first 12 months of launching, mymuesli had more than 1 million euros ($1.3 million) in revenue. "We achieved that easily," Max said. "We were almost profitable from the start."

The company has kept growing with similar ease: mymuesli now ships to five countries across Europe (Germany, Austria, Switzerland, the United Kingdom and the Netherlands), has production facilities in two countries, employs more than 100 people and has offices and brick-and-mortar stores in Germany and Switzerland. It has even invested what Max calls "a lot" of money in building the world's first-ever fully automated

CONTINUES

CONTINUED
custom cereal mixer, which started production in 2012. If the mixer is as effective as it promises to be, mymuesli could slash the cost of custom cereal, which it has already priced as low as high-end in-store cereals, and make it as cheap as a box of mass-produced Kellogg's Corn Flakes.

So what exactly happened between Levi's shutting down Original Spin in 2003 and launching Curve ID in 2010 to make the outcomes so different? Over the first decade of the new millennium, the problems that the CIY business model had have vanished.

Here's the picture today:

1. **Fast internet connections.** Two-thirds of Americans have fast broadband or wireless connections that can handle create-it-yourself Web design tools perfectly. Meanwhile, the percentage of Americans who use the internet increased from 50 percent in 2001 to 78 percent in 2011.[8]

2. **Cheaper website design.** Ten years ago, developing a website with a create-it-yourself function ("Build-a-Bear," "Customize-a-Car," "Create-a-Bag," etc.) cost around $1 million and took nine months to build. Now the same website can be built in one month for just $5,000.[9] This development has come thanks to advanced template-based Web design companies like California-based Treehouse Logic and Vienna-based cyLEDGE. As a result, custom products don't have to cost a premium just to pay the Web designers. Configurators are now so much fun to use that companies are launching them even when direct sales from them are impossible. For example, in 2011, when Boeing unveiled the 787 Dreamliner, its newest commercial jet, the aircraft manufacturer also launched (as part of the fanfare for the new jet) a customizer on its website that allowed anyone to design the exterior of their very own 787 Dreamliner.[10] What's more, tiny companies

can now use online marketplaces, like arts-and-crafts website Etsy, to sell custom products easily (albeit without the appealing Web visual).

3. **Confidence in online purchasing.** Until recently, the vast majority of consumers lacked the confidence to buy products online. It took years, and the tried-and-tested emergence of trusted brand names like PayPal, McAfee and VeriSign, for consumers to feel comfortable putting their credit card and bank details online. Today, buying online is normal. During the first half of 2011, roughly $1 out of every $10 consumers spent was spent online. Total online sales in 2010 amounted to more than $142.5 billion—a full 10 percent increase from 2009 alone.

4. **Internet access almost everywhere.** Americans now are connected more than ever, with access to the internet 24/7 from almost everywhere: at work, at coffee shops, in the car, bus and train—even in bed. More than 50 percent of American consumers will have a smartphone before the end of 2012.[11] It is not surprising, therefore, that the amount of time Americans spend online has increased by 121 percent in the last five years (between 2005 and 2010) to an average of 13 hours a week per person.[12] For the up-and-coming generation, the number is much higher. Young people between the ages of 8 and 18 spend an average of 7.5 hours online every day.[13]

5. **The internet allowed niche advertising.** The widespread use of the internet has also enabled customization companies to reach their individual targeted markets through search engines, search ads, banner ads, niche blogs, viral apps and social media sites at reasonable or no cost.

6. **More streamlined shipping methods.** Fully automated shipping software (for producing labels, integrating mass uploads of shipping addresses, etc.) that was once only available to large corporations is now available to small businesses through FedEx, USPS and UPS, thanks to revolutionary improvements in

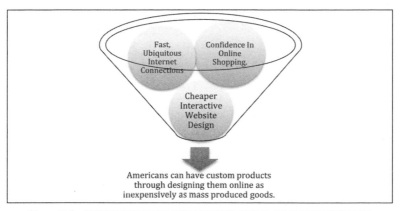

Figure 2.6 KEY INTERNET-RELATED TECHNOLOGICAL ADVANCEMENTS THAT HAVE MADE THE CUSTOM REVOLUTION POSSIBLE

software programs. This means that even small businesses can now ship single, customized orders without incurring sky-high labor costs in their shipping departments.

The 21st Century—CIY Customization Starts Taking Over

As a result of all these factors, fully customized goods of all shapes and sizes are now, for the first time ever, becoming available at roughly the same price and high quality as mass-produced ones. Examples are everywhere. Zazzle and CustomInk sell high-quality custom T-shirts for roughly the same price you'd pay at stores like Target for mass-produced T-shirts. Blue Nile and Gemvara sell custom jewelry for the same price (or sometimes even cheaper) than you'd pay at a shopping mall jeweler. For BMW, forget mass production altogether; the prestigious carmaker now routinely makes all its new cars to order. Coca-Cola recently invested $100 million developing a custom drink maker, called Coca-Cola Freestyle, that allows consumers to design their own sodas (by mixing and matching other Coca-Cola–owned drinks) for the same price as a standard drink. Frommer's sells completely customized travel guides (including personalized covers) for roughly the same price as its standard selection of guides. L'Oreal, the giant French makeup company, has an entire website devoted to personalized cosmetics.[14]

The list goes on and on, and it stars many smaller names too. Boutique handbag makers, like Laudi Vidni and Anna Street Studio, sell one-of-a-kind designer bags for the same price as high-end, mass-produced ones. Innovative online tailors, like Proper Cloth and Solosso, tailor-make men's shirts for the same price you'd pay at a department store off the rack. Fun-filled online clothing stores, like FashionPlaytes and Customized Girl, allow kids to design their own clothes for the same price as clothes at Gap Kids. Villy Customs produces completely custom bicycles for the same amount as a standard Schwinn bike.

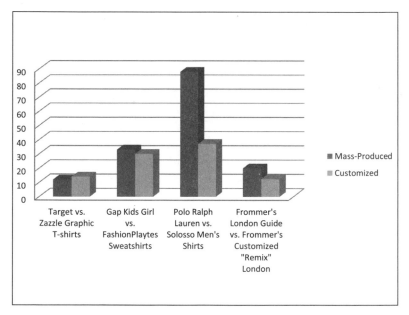

Figure 2.7   MASS-PRODUCED GOODS vs. CUSTOM GOODS (in US $)

Go online today and you'll find more than 700 total customization companies, offering goods of all shapes and sizes.[15] If you know where to look, you can buy *affordable, customized* engagement rings, kitten heels, autobiographies, novels, suitcases, protein powder, beef jerky, pet food, furniture, mosaics, music, iPhone covers, safari holidays, news and even true love (thanks to the surge of customized online dating services). It is impossible to stress strongly enough just how recent a phenomenon this really is and how much opportunity for growth there is in customization. According to research from academics at MIT's Smart Customization Group, roughly 85 percent of customizing companies have launched in the last five years, with almost 30 percent having launched in the last 12 months.

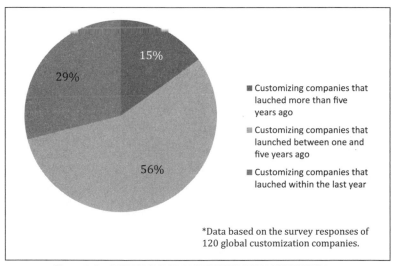

Figure 2.8   RECENT SURGE IN CUSTOMIZATION COMPANIES*

What Customization Means for the Economy

With customization being such an enormous growth market, it promises to represent an important percentage of some of America's biggest industries very soon. Frank Piller, the head of MIT's Smart Customization Group, estimates that within the next decade as much as 15 percent of the clothing Americans buy will be customized, and that as much as 5 percent of the manufactured food and drink items they buy will be customized. These statistics might seem small percentage-wise. But in absolute numbers, they're enormous. Americans spend roughly $250 billion a year on clothing and roughly $1 trillion a year on manufactured (processed and/or pre-made) food and drinks. This means that by 2020 the annual market for customized clothing will be worth an estimated $37.5 billion and that the annual market for customized food and drinks will be worth an estimated $50 billion.

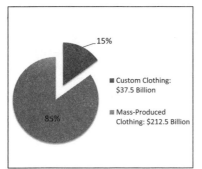

Figure 2.9 ESTIMATED VALUE OF U.S. CUSTOM CLOTHING INDUSTRY IN 2020
Source: MIT Smart Customization Group

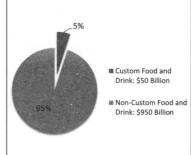

Figure 2.10 ESTIMATED VALUE OF AMERICAN CUSTOM FOOD AND DRINK INDUSTRY IN 2020
Source: MIT Smart Customization Group

■ Investors Go Custom

With that kind of backdrop, it's not surprising that smart investors are going custom. Exciting examples are everywhere and started appearing around 2008. In the 12 months between August 2008 and August 2009 alone, six custom apparel and accessory firms, including FashionPlaytes and J. Hilburn, together received more than $100 million in private equity, venture capital (VC) and angel financing from investors.[16,17] In 2010, Skinit, a company that makes custom cases for electronic devices like mobile phones, tablets and laptops (and has distribution deals with such big names as HP and Microsoft), raised $60 million in venture capital funding, and in 2011 was ranked 25th on *Forbes'* annual list of America's Most Promising Companies. In 2012 Gemvara, an online-only custom jewelry dealer, brought the amount of funding it has received from venture capitalists (VCs) up to $51 million.

Josh Elman, a principal at booming Silicon Valley venture capital firm Greylock Partners (which has $1 billion in funds and has invested in such powerhouse companies as Facebook, LinkedIn and Pandora), is extremely interested in companies with custom business models. "We've thought a lot about personalization," he told me when I interviewed him at a customization conference in late 2011. "What's interesting about Pandora and Facebook is that they are [delivering] hundreds of millions of custom experiences every minute of every day," he said, referring to Pandora's custom radio stations and Facebook's custom newsfeeds. "Instead of going to a shopping store with inventory of thousands, now we're all [going to shopping stores with] infinite inventories." The possibilities for financial payoff are incredible, said Josh. "Public markets are now valuing customization...[and] personalization is disrupting many long-standing industries."

CASE STUDY: SHUTTERFLY

If you still have any doubts that customization is the future of business, look no further than Shutterfly, the custom photo gift company, which climbed to a company valuation of approximately $1 billion while Eastman Kodak Co., the century-old star of everything photo, filed for bankruptcy protection—all because Shutterfly does customization right.

When Silicon Valley entrepreneur Jim Clark started Shutterfly in December 1999, his idea was to give American consumers the ability to print photographs from their digital cameras. Back then only a tiny number of Americans had digital cameras. With a simple two-megapixel camera costing as much as $800, it's not hard to see why. But Jim was convinced that the world would switch to digital; in retrospect, his prediction couldn't have been more prescient.

But here's what's interesting: It wasn't Jim's early move into the digital photo space alone that turned Shutterfly into the success it is today. In fact, despite his foresight, Shutterfly faltered massively during the dot-com bust. The reason the company survived, and ultimately beat out the big competitors in the space, is that it offered a level of customization that its competitors weren't offering. Around 2004, when it became clear to everyone (and not just Jim) that Americans were, in fact, swapping film for digital, hundreds of companies rushed into the digital photo printing space.

At the time, Shutterfly was far from a household name. The company had just $50 million in annual revenue in 2004 and was barely turning a profit. Meanwhile, Kodak—the age-old king of American photography—had, by 2005, surged to the No. 1 spot in U.S. digital camera sales and was pulling in $5.7 billion annually. Back then, if you had to bet on which company would be filing for bankruptcy protection in 2012, the smart bet would have been Shutterfly by a mile. But, of course, history tells a different story.

Although Kodak had embraced digital cameras, the company failed to see what people would want to use them for. Kodak kept thinking consumers would still want standard 4x6 photographs. In 2005 Shutterfly hired eBay's customer acquisition guru, Jeffrey Housenbold, to take over as its new CEO. Jeff

CONTINUES

CONTINUED

had a different idea, which he told me when I spoke to him in the spring of 2012:

> When I walked in [as CEO of Shutterfly], we were largely undifferentiated from the competition. It was all about 4x6 prints and price. We were not helping people do more with their images and memories. We were much more along the old paradigm, which was: Drop off a roll of film, develop prints and place them in clear sleeves for users to put in a binder on a bookshelf. I brought a different perspective and said, "My wife and I use Shutterfly to stay connected in this dual-income, geographically fragmented, time-compressed society where we have friends and family all over the world." I thought of it as a social connection and a way to share life's memories with friends and family.

Shutterfly dropped the "photo printers" tagline and started calling itself an "Internet-based social expression and personal publishing service." And while Kodak remained focused on the old 4x6 photo for the bookshelf binder, Shutterfly turned its eye to more customized and lucrative products like custom calendars, custom greeting cards, custom photo books, custom mugs and custom mouse pads. The company also started putting an enormous value on gaining the trust and loyalty of their customers. Unlike many of its competitors, Shutterfly never deleted a single photo its users uploaded, regardless of whether that customer bought anything. As Jeff said, "We have always had this customer-centric approach, where it is not about photos and it is not about this month's revenue. It is about a lifelong relationship."

Jeff's vision paid off. In January 2011 Shutterfly became one of the world's first true customizers to break the $1 billion mark for a public company valuation. Soon after, in January 2012, the less customizing Kodak filed for bankruptcy protection; two months later, the once-iconic photo company sold its online arm, the Kodak Gallery (complete with 75 million users), to Shutterfly for $23.8 million. "We're really a David versus Goliath success story," Jeff told me. "We started out competing against Hallmark, Kodak, the list goes on and on . . . and we've emerged to be the largest and most profitable enterprise."

For more information about the companies discussed throughout this book, visit CustomNation.com/Companies.

CHAPTER 3

Custom Generation
Why the 21st Century's Consumers Want Custom Everything

I like to think I'm a pretty well-read guy. I read *The New York Times* and *The Wall Street Journal* every day. And I was a business major at USC, so instead of listening to music in the car, I always put on the latest business book I've downloaded onto my iPhone. But do you know what the first piece of news I check when I wake up in the morning is? My Facebook newsfeed. The second thing? Twitter. And that is exactly the same thing that all of my friends who are my age (29, by the way) do when they wake up. Personalized news—about people we know and things we care about—is simply more relevant to us than the cover story of *The New York Times*, so it's where we go first.

My friends and I don't have a custom expectation just when it comes to news—we have it in every single facet of our lives. We expect personal restaurant recommendations from our iPhone apps, custom directions from our GPS devices and constant individualized newsfeeds (care of Facebook and other social networking sites) to such a degree that we'd rather sacrifice our sense of smell than our smartphones (according to an informal poll of friends).

I was talking about all of this recently with my friend Sebastian, a 25-year-old native Californian who was in the same fraternity I was in at

USC a few years after me, and as soon as I floated my poll question, he summed up my underlying point in just a few gestures. First, he pointed down to the custom Zazzle T-shirt he was wearing (with the slogan: "Guns Don't Kill People. Ninjas Kill People."), then he took a sip of his custom Starbucks coffee (a "short double red-eye") and finally he headed out to work *at 3 p.m.* to his current short-contract job as a Web designer for an internet startup that allows customized hours. "It's not that I don't like one-size-fits-all stuff and mainstream 9-to-5 routines," he said as he left. "I just like *my* stuff and *my* schedule better." (Incidentally, he said he'd sacrifice his sense of smell *and* taste if it meant keeping his iPhone.)

Sebastian isn't alone. In fact, his completely customized lifestyle is typical of our entire generation. Millennials—generally defined as people born between 1978 and 2000, who came of age after the start of the new millennium—have come to expect customization in everything we do and buy. Instead of driving identical cars (like our parents with their 1960s VW Beetles), we purchase custom, built-to-order Scions on the company's customizing website. (Scion is the most popular car brand in America with buyers aged 18 to 27,[1] and I believe its enormous popularity is because of the way it encourages consumers to customize their cars.) Instead of listening to entire CDs, we tune in only to completely customized playlists care of iTunes on our iPods, or listen to customized radio stations on Pandora. Instead of watching television, we consume on-demand digital recordings on Netflix and YouTube. (The last time Sebastian watched a TV commercial was during the Super Bowl.)

If you look closely, there isn't a single aspect of millennial lives that isn't customized. We design avatar alter egos in virtual worlds like Ever-Quest (a popular online role-playing game), we get custom dating recommendations from matchmaking websites, we have custom sneakers on our feet, custom sweatshirts on our backs, custom sleeves for our laptops and iPhones packed full of our favorite songs, shows and photos. As a group, we even customize our bodies: 38 percent of 18- to 29-year-olds have at least one tattoo; 69 percent of those have two or more.[2] My coauthor is also a millennial. She was born in 1980 and has two totally customized tattoos, including one of her husband's initials.

■What This Means for Business

All of this matters *a lot* for anyone who wants to be successful in business today ... and tomorrow. During the past 50 years, every good marketer's goal was to hone in on what baby boomers wanted and deliver it (so Bob Dylan albums went platinum five times and flower-power VW Beetles became the best-selling cars of all time). In short, my parents' generation has pretty much single-handedly driven the economy for as long as most people can remember. But their choke hold on consumerism is coming to an end. Boomers are hitting their golden years with underfunded pensions and homes worth much less than they expected. As a result, they're cutting back on spending like there *is* a tomorrow.

[M]y parents' generation has pretty much single-handedly driven the economy for as long as most people can remember. But their choke hold on consumerism is coming to an end.

Generation X, the generation between the boomers and the millennials, was never large enough to break boomer-centric marketing.[3] But the millennials—the boomers' children—sure are. They're starting to hit their 30s—and they're spending. Consider these two stats: Today, there are roughly 75 million baby boomers in the United States, and because they are aging, their numbers are in decline. By contrast, there are *already* more than 95 million millennials,[4] and thanks to immigration, the number of those in this age group is on the rise.

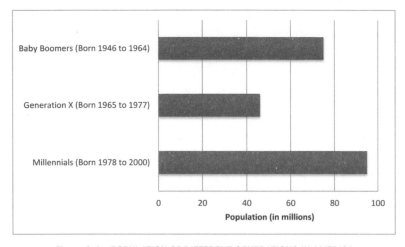

Figure 3.1   POPULATION OF DIFFERENT GENERATIONS IN AMERICA
Source: Generation We (gen-we.com) and *Time* magazine

Frank Piller, the head of MIT's Smart Customization Group and a professor at one of Europe's leading technology colleges (the RWTH Aachen University in Germany), is one of the best-known professors of customization in the world. He has been teaching his students about the potential of large-scale customization for *two decades*. But here's what's interesting: Frank told me that it has only been for the last few years that he doesn't have to explain to his students why customization is such an appealing business model. "I never get the 'so what' anymore," Frank said. "My students don't see customization as special any longer; they just expect it." Previously when he had brought up the idea of customized goods, students discussed why consumers would like it or how much of a premium they would be willing to pay for it.

Looking back at his 20 years in the world of customization, he said, "We've been talking about the potential customization has to revolutionize business for a long time, but it feels like it has finally arrived." One of the areas where this evolution is most obvious is in the ubiquitous way that online retailers are now *typically* using personalization techniques to market their goods to individual consumers, by, for example, offering deals, discounts or free shipping specific to individuals' preferences. Indeed, a full 50 percent of the largest online retailers in the United States used some customized marketing and sales techniques in 2011, compared with around a third the year before, according to Internet Retailer's Top 500 Guide. To do this, these online retailers are paying specialty software companies like MyBuys and Monetate to help them analyze customer information.[5]

"My students don't see customization as special any longer; they just expect it."

—Frank Piller, head of MIT's Smart Customization Group

■ If You Can, You Will

Millennials' embrace of customization has commanded a lot of sociological attention. Many social science academics, such as San Diego State University's Jean Twenge (author of *Generation Me*), trace the generation's desire to get exactly what they want (and feel unhappy with anything less) to the "entitled" or "narcissistic" way that we as a generation were raised—getting to choose, for example, what to have for dinner, instead of having to eat whatever was on the table or go to bed hungry the way kids in the 1950s did.[6]

But there's a more intuitive reason—one that many people who study consumer trends (myself included) think is the real truth. We believe the drive for custom goods is simply an inherent part of being human—one that we had to suppress during the 20th century because of the economic convenience of mass production. Bob Marino, the thought-provoking CEO of the giant customizing company CafePress (worth more than a quarter of a billion dollars) and a self-described "advance scout for Generation X," told us that he believes the reason for the explosion of demand for custom goods is simply that it is now possible.

"That's how human beings are wired," he said. "We are individuals, not genetic copies of one another. . . . It has always been true that if you had the ability to get custom goods, you would want to."

> We believe the drive for custom goods is simply an inherent part of being human—one that we had to suppress during the 20th century because of the economic convenience of mass production.

Bob's theory is certainly empirically true. The rich—who could afford things like custom suits and homes—have *always* bought them. Ginanne Brownell, a London-based journalist who has written extensively about luxury trends for publications like *Newsweek*, said that in the world of high-end purchases, individuality and customization have always been key catchphrases. "The ultra-wealthy spend a lot on personalization," she said. "They'll appoint top perfumeries to make custom perfumes designed for their skin, commission authors to write their biographies and hire professional artists to paint murals in their baby nurseries."

When custom is possible, we love opting for it. Millennials, like the privileged rich of the 20th century, are buying custom goods because they *can*. If previous generations had those tools at their fingertips, they would have done it too.

Growing Up on Customization

There is already evidence that in the future, society will require even more customization. The generation growing up right after the millennials doesn't just expect customization; they are completely at one with it—almost from birth. It is kind of odd to think of them as a consumer group because we're talking about kids under the age of 13. But they aren't just children with tiny iPad-tapping fingers—they are the future of retail. For proof, you need only look at how effortlessly 8-year-old girls create their own Barbie dolls online—selecting their dolls' skin color, outfits and accessories, care of Mattel's Barbie Styled by Me customizing website that also allows girls to create their own miniature custom slogan T-shirts for their Barbies.

And even younger kids are getting comfortable with customizing their purchases. At a recent cocktail party, my sister's friend Melanie Riker was talking about her 4-year-old son Aiden's adoration of Porsche's customizer website, which lets him (and his dad) custom design their own unique Porsches. "I have to watch him really closely when he plays on it," she joked. "I'm worried he'll accidently push the BUY button and we'll get a Porsche delivered to our driveway and a $200,000 bill in the mailbox!"

BIG IN GERMANY: MILLENNIALS IN EUROPE LOVE CUSTOMIZING TOO

The United States isn't the only nation in the world that's going custom. In fact, customization is one of the biggest business trends across the developed world. In Europe, the unquestionable heart of the movement toward "custom everything" is Germany. And one of that country's biggest success stories is the chocolate customizer chocri.

In 2008, chocri launched with one aim: to offer customers completely customizable chocolate bars. You can create a chocolate bar filled with anything from lavender buds and candied rose petals to cayenne pepper and real gold flakes. Setting in motion a global craving for custom chocolate, chocri's innovative business model was a true trailblazer. Today there are dozens of companies around the world with the same delectable business model, including the excellent Chocomize in the United States.

Just two years after setting up shop online, chocri made another trailblazing move when it became the world's first-ever customized food producer to accept a partial buyout from a mainstream food producer. In 2010, Ritter Sport paid more than 1 million euros ($1.3 million) for 33 percent of chocri, which now sells more than 60,000 bars per month[7] and has expanded into England and the United States. The investment from Ritter came with advice too. Since getting Ritter on board, chocri has been able to slash its costs by 30 percent.

CONTINUES

CONTINUED

Carmen Magar brought chocri to the United States as the CEO of the company's American business, based in New York. Carmen and I talked about the reasons that custom food is becoming such a success story. "In general, people are a lot more conscious of what they eat than they used to be," she mused. "We now have functional foods that we eat to improve health." With certain food items, like chocolate, she added, the huge gift market also plays a role—chocri allows customers to design bars to woo their loved ones via special ingredients and by naming the bars themselves. And, according to Carmen, around half of chocri's customers use the package to say something really special: "I Love You."

◼ Custom Lifestyles

Customization isn't simply revolutionizing consumer behavior for the youngest generations of Americans. Those who came of age in the new millennium exhibit an appetite for choice and customization across *all* aspects of their lives. At home millennials are, in effect, customizing their relationships and family structures to suit themselves, instead of adhering to one-size-fits-all tradition. In 1950, 63 percent of families were "traditional"—that is, couples were married, dads worked outside of the house and moms labored at home. Today, the choices of acceptable lifestyles have mushroomed, leading the number of "traditional" families to drop to a tiny minority of just 17 percent.[8] As of 2006, more than a third of millennials who are moms had their babies out of wedlock.[9]

Even those who end up opting for marriage are hoping to bring a larger capacity for customization to that institution. A July 2011 survey by the Public Religion Research Institute found that 62 percent of 18- to 29-year-olds believe that whether couples are heterosexual or homosexual, they should be allowed to marry. By contrast, only 47 percent of the general public want to add the choice of same-sex partners to the institution of marriage and just 31 percent of people over 65 want to see a change.[10]

Millennials also want to customize their working lives to suit their overall lifestyles, instead of forcing life to fit into work. Only 15 percent of millennials rank "having a high-paying career" as "one of the most important things in their lives," according to a 2011 Pew Research poll. The top thing that matters to them? "Being a good parent," which got a heartwarming 52 percent of the vote. To that end, while 70 percent of baby boomers care about achieving a work-life balance in their careers, a full 92 percent of millennials want a work-life balance. Cathy Benko, the author of *Mass Career Customization: Aligning the Workplace with Today's Nontraditional Workforce* and vice chairman at the consulting firm Deloitte, told me this is all part of the same process. "If you can customize jeans, sneakers, music and M&M's, then why not careers?"[11]

Customization is such an integral part of millennials' approach to the world that it has even begun influencing how we teach them, and ultimately, how they will teach the generation after them. New York's Department of Education is running a custom math program for middle schoolers, which it calls the School of One. As the name suggests, the School of One offers completely customized mathematics classes for each of its students. Instead of getting "tracked" on math schedules with 50 or 100 other students of similar (but never quite the same) abilities, teenagers in the School of One get their own individual lesson schedules, which the school fashionably calls "playlists," consisting of a combination of virtual online tutoring, math-based video games, computer worksheets and small group lessons with a teacher. In traditional math classrooms, teachers progress at a mid-class pace—boring the fastest students and baffling the slowest—but at the School of One, students progress exactly when they have personally mastered each lesson.

The School of One program is proving to be such a success that New York's Department of Education has expanded it to three schools in the last two years, with plans to more than double that in September 2012. It is not alone. There are dozens of other similarly customized education platforms catching on all over the United States, including New York City's Innovation Zone and YouTube's universal Khan Academy. Ben Pomerantz, a lecturer at the USC School of Social Work, who brought the School of One and the Khan Academy to my attention, told me that customization is having such an enormous impact on how educators are thinking about teaching that the topic deserves a whole chapter in this book. "It's one of the most discussed topics in education right now," he said.

Interestingly, the experts I spoke with in almost every major social arena, from education to politics to religion, said that the ethos of customization is also revolutionizing their fields. Just one more example: Rebecca Voorwinde, a friend of mine who works for a leading Jewish nonprofit organization, said that younger American Jews are "customizing" the religion to make it relevant and personal for themselves. "There are tons of online resources for DIY Judaism," Rebecca said. "Young Jews can go on haggadot.com and design their own personalized books to use at Passover, including contemporary texts, artwork and video clips; and there are projects like the Sabbath Manifesto that put a modern and customized spin on traditional Sabbath observance. Instead of the strict rules of no work and attending synagogue, emphasis is placed on bringing balance to one's life through a weekly technology detox."

For more information about the companies discussed throughout this book, visit CustomNation.com/Companies.

RENTAL CUSTOMIZATION

Several excellent new books, including Rachel Botsman and Roo Rogers' *What's Mine Is Yours* and Lisa Gansky's *The Mesh: Why the Future of Business Is Sharing*, have convincingly argued that the future of commerce will be all about "sharing." Here's the argument: In the modern internet age, people are able to conveniently rent all sorts of things for all sorts of periods of time, from bicycles to rides to work to strangers' guest rooms for vacations, leading to a massive rise in people effectively "sharing" goods rather than buying them outright.

CONTINUES

CONTINUED

While I agree that this phenomenon is big and growing, I would argue that even this is an offshoot of millennials' comfort level with custom everything. While the term *sharing* has been widely adopted to describe this phenomenon, what we're seeing with most of these platforms is actually not sharing in the classic sense of the word at all—rather it is *individualized renting*.

A woman can now rent out her apartment in New York for the week she is going to be in the Bahamas, instead of letting it sit empty. A commuter can rent a car or bicycle just for the hours he drives to and from work, instead of buying one and letting it sit unused in the parking lot of his office building every day. Millennials are recognizing the individual way that they use their goods and either turning the time they aren't using their goods into a source of income or saving money by not buying at all.

What's brand-new about this is not the "sharing" (capitalism has, of course, always been big on rentals) but that these new companies provide rental experiences that are specifically customized to meet the exact time and usage needs of the renter and the owner. This is a new economy of *usage customization*.

CHAPTER  4

The Paradox of Choice

No book on 20th century manufacturing is ever complete without a nod to Henry Ford's classic 1922 line on the wonders of mass production: "Any customer can have a car painted any color that he wants, so long as it's black." But fittingly for a company that was on the cutting edge of bringing mass production into the mainstream, the Ford Motor Co. is now on the cutting edge of going totally customized.

Forget black. If you go online to buy a Ford today, the company's flagship Mustang homepage reads: "All Legend. Zero Compromise. Dream Up Your Ultimate Mustang. Launch the Customizer."[1] The Customizer delivers exactly what the word promises. Click through it and you're greeted with the choice of four different Mustang models to use as your base car under the headline "Do Mess with Perfection." Beyond that, there are too many choices to count, allowing you to create your perfect car by combining hundreds of different options, including 23 different wheels, six decklids and dozens of door and hood designs, like orange flames and cobra snakeheads. On the Customizer, your Mustang's color isn't just a choice of many—it's completely create-it-yourself, care of three coordinated color bars that allow you to craft your own unique color and then save it. It almost makes you feel sorry for black.

Figure 4.1   THEN . . . AUTOMOBILE—BLACK FORD
Source: Copyright Ford Motor Company (Ford.wieck.com)

Figure 4.2   AND NOW . . . MUSTANG CUSTOMIZER
Source: Copyright Ford Motor Company (Ford.wieck.com)

The Paradox of Choice: When More Is Not Better

For marketing experts, however, the custom Mustang's success begs a very
important question: How do they make customizing cars so much *fun*? Red

or silver? Flames or cobra? Convertible or sunroof? In the science of sales, too much choice is actually considered a bad thing. When confronted with a plethora of options, consumers often get overwhelmed, worry about making the wrong choice and end up choosing nothing at all—frozen by indecision or exhausted by it all taking too much time.

Sheena Iyengar, a professor at Columbia Business School, conducted *the* definitive experiment on this subject. In it, her researchers set up a jam sampling table at a high-end grocery store in California. On the first day of the experiment, they offered shoppers a tantalizing 24 different jams to taste. On the second day, they offered just six. Shoppers who tasted jams received a coupon to buy any jam of the same brand in the store. The results were stark: When there were just six jams on the table, shoppers bought *ten times more*—only 3 percent of the shoppers who tasted at the 24-jam table went on to buy a jar, while 30 percent of those who tasted at the six-jam sampling went on to purchase a jar.[2]

This result seems irrational. You should be more likely to find something you like from a fourfold larger sample, not less likely. But choice can be paralyzing, and not just in jams—in everything. Similar experiments have been conducted on everyone from students to chocolate eaters, and the results are always the same. When students are offered a choice of six topics to write about for extra credit, for example, they are more likely to write a paper than students given the choice of 30 topics. When an appliance store has a single item on display for a large discount in the window, sales are better than when they have two different items on sale at the same big discount. On the face of it, you'd think that more choices would mean more takers, but in reality, more choices mean *fewer* buyers, hence the "paradox."

In all likelihood, you've even had this experience. When you walk into a grocery store and see 14 types of milk or 16 brands of facial tissue, how do you choose? Scanning for color, quality and per-item price is almost always too time-consuming across a seeming football-field-length shelf offering a million types of the same product. Typically, we all use a shortcut to make a choice: brand. We feel that Kleenex, for example, has a good reputation and knows how many tissues we want per box and what scents smell good. They're not the cheapest, but they're reasonably priced (at least we have that feeling, usually without actually checking the price). If we stopped and weighed all our options for everything on our shopping list, it would take all day. Or we might just get exhausted and give up. We need a filter for our choices.

Overcoming the Problem of Too Much Choice

The paradox of choice obviously poses an enormous potential problem for companies with CIY business models. Customization is all about choice; so how do customizers keep their shoppers from freezing with indecision—or getting tired and giving up—over whether to go with blue or silver or red or . . . well, you get the picture. In theory, of course, we love the idea of getting to choose and are often unhappy with the limited offerings of the big brands. But the reality is different.

Hundreds of customizers have run into exactly the same problem. We've all spent valuable time and money overcoming the paradox of choice. And here's what's fascinating: As I did the interviews for this book, I found that every single successful customization company (whether producing cars, jewelry, photo books or computers) had discovered the *same two rules* for beating the challenge of choice.

The Rules for Overcoming the Paradox of Choice

1. Never give your customers too many choices.
Large customizing companies typically have employees called "choice architects" whose full-time job is to make sure customers' choices are

perfect (offering, for example, only choices that go well together) and the experience of choosing is fun. Vistaprint's CEO Robert Keane also pointed out that limiting consumers' choices is vital from the perspective of making production cost-effective: "You destroy the economics of mass customization with too many choices. If you don't standardize the choices, you can't automate and standardize the production. Then you're forcing yourself back into traditional customization, not mass customization."

2. Give your customers the option of choosing a *finished design* as a starting point.

When Laura Kofoid, a Harvard Business School graduate, launched her custom designer handbag line Laudi Vidni (the brand name spells "individual" backward) in 2002, her idea was to let consumers design everything about their bags. But she found growth from that model difficult. "There was an idea [back then] that if you gave consumers the chance to customize, they would jump at the opportunity," she told me. "I'd ask my Web designers how many color and stitching options I should give my customers, and they'd say, '*Everything!*'" Over time she realized that "everything" was too overwhelming. So Laura started designing bags that her customers could use as starting points for designing their own bags. This "inspiration," as Laura called it, has been a key factor in pushing her business to the big time. While the last 10 years were a struggle, she was anticipating more than $1 million sales in 2012. "I still don't really believe it myself," she told me in a whisper when we were discussing how much the company had boomed.

▊ Payoff: The 'I Did It Myself' Phenomenon

At this point, you're probably wondering why you should even bother with offering customization. If customers find choosing so difficult and overwhelming, why not just push-market a single mass-produced item? Well, here's the answer . . .

[I]t is an established fact in behavioral psychology that people absolutely love things they've toiled to create.

Anyone who has tasted a tomato grown in her own garden knows it tastes better than the store-bought version. Indeed, it is an established fact in behavioral psychology that people absolutely love things they've toiled to create. So when customizing companies do a good job of giving customers an enjoyable experience of codesign, consumers' appreciation of— and willingness to spend money on—the end result exceeds mass production's wildest fantasies. At tasting events that Crushpad, a custom winemaker, holds for clients, 80 percent believe *their own wine* is the very best. The emotional resonance of the items can't be beat either. I've personally talked to dozens of customers of Shutterfly and I don't know if I've ever seen such a devoted customer group. One friend of mine told me, "Shutterfly *was* Christmas for me last year. Every gift I gave—photo books, personalized mugs and calendars—I made on their website, and my family loved the items so much that most of them actually teared up when I gave them their gifts."

Dan Ariely, one of the world's foremost behavioral economists, said that when companies do a good job of customizing, this kind of powerful emotional connection with consumers isn't just enviable, it's *normal*. Dan would know—he is the James B. Duke Professor of Psychology and Behavioral Economics at Duke University and the author of three *New York Times* bestsellers about why people act the way they do, including 2008's runaway hit *Predictably Irrational: The Hidden Forces That Shape Our Decisions*. In addition to all that, Dan has also carved out a front-row seat for watching how people decide what to buy, and how much to spend on it, by doing hundreds of scintillating scientific experiments on everyone from everyday consumers to elite college students.[3]

I interviewed Dan for this book and he said that his studies repeatedly show that the kind of passionate customer base that companies such as Shutterfly and Crushpad have is typical when consumers imprint their own ideas on to products. "The moment you believe people are different, you [also] know that people want individual customization. . . . There's no other way to think about it," said Dan.

In his studies, Dan has gotten people to build all sorts of random things—like origami frogs and Lego helicopters—and then rate how nice they think the things they built are compared to similar objects built by others. Here's how Dan summarized his findings: "The first thing we found was if there was an origami that you built and an origami that somebody else built, you think that yours is much, much more beautiful. Not only is it more beautiful, you're willing to pay much more for it. . . ."

The studies backing this up are fascinating.[4] In one experiment, Dan and his colleagues broke their test subjects into two groups. People in the first group were each given one already-built IKEA storage box; people in the second group were each given the materials and directions to build the same box and asked to build it. After all boxes were built, test subjects were asked how much they would be willing to pay for the boxes to take them home. Those who had put in their own labor to build the finished box were willing to pay 78 cents for the box. Those who didn't build were only willing to pay 48 cents.

What's more, when test subjects were given a task with a more creative slant—making origami birds and frogs—the difference between how much they valued the product and how much others (who hadn't done the paper-folding themselves) valued the creations increased dramatically. While the do-it-yourself group was willing to pay an average of 23 cents to take home their origami creations, participants in an outside control group who were asked how much they would pay to take home these same origami creations bid an average of just 5 cents. As Dan and his cowriters concluded, "While the non-builders saw the amateurish creations as nearly worthless crumpled paper, our builders imbued their origami with value."[5]

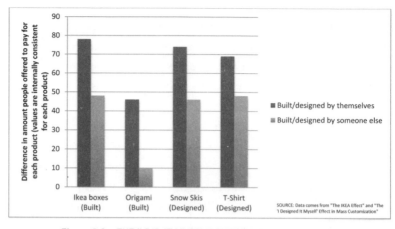

Figure 4.3   THE 'I DID IT MYSELF' PHENOMENON IN NUMBERS

This phenomenon is also visible even when people don't put physical labor into building something but rather place designs on pre-made objects online, which is the dominant business model of many customizing companies like Zazzle and CafePress. One such experiment, led by Nikolaus Franke, a professor of entrepreneurship and innovation at the Vienna University of Economics and Business, looked at how online self-design influenced the value of snow skis. For the study, Franke broke his test subjects into two groups. The first group was given the opportunity to virtually design a pair of blank snow skis, choosing from a set of patterns and images. The second group was given the opportunity to choose a pair of skis from a set of professional designs. Those who designed their own skis were willing to pay *nearly double* the amount for them as those who chose from professional designs.[6,7]

The psychological phenomenon behind this—sometimes called the 'I Did It Myself' Effect—is, in essence, the same one that is at play with parents and their children. When new parents tell endless stories about their babies rolling or babbling, they really do believe these stories are endlessly fascinating and unimaginably fantastic, even if it bores the rest of us. Through pouring ourselves into raising our children, we view our children as the cutest, most captivating, most adorable people on the planet, and we think everyone else will feel the same way about them.

Through pouring ourselves into raising our children, we view our children as the cutest, most captivating, most adorable people on the planet, and we think everyone else will feel the same way about them.

In exactly this same way, when we have poured ourselves into creating an object—be it a bottle of wine, a silver necklace or, yes, even a jar of custom jam (such as one by Jam Anarchy)—we believe that object to be the best there is of its kind in the entire world. One Crushpad customer, Rick Speer, even told us that when he saw the Crushpad wine that he'd spent months crafting finally being bottled and put in cases, that it was "like giving birth." Eat your heart out, mass production.

In practice, Dan says that, in order for businesses to capitalize on this "I Did It Myself" idea, it is vital to strike a balance between asking customers to do too little and asking them to do too much:

There are two types of customization: customization that people know about, and customization that people don't know about. If you go to a shoe store and they measure your foot, you know you're getting a custom service as you've taken the time to get your foot measured. [By contrast,] if Amazon gives a book recommendation, that's a kind of under-the-rug hidden customization. Amazon doesn't know what you really like; they guess. This under-the-rug customization is very good for matching consumers with products they'll probably like without the customer having to spend their own time on it—the company does the work, you reap the benefit.

But that's not the maximum value. [It takes customers putting in] individualized effort to achieve the maximum value. But that involves work and challenges. [It can become] too laborious and painful [for consumers]. There is a trade-off between being overwhelmed with choice and tired from all the work around that, and actually getting the ability to make what you really want. The goal is to master that balancing act: to pull in the customer without tiring them out.

For more information about the companies discussed throughout this book, visit CustomNation.com/Companies.

CASE STUDY OF CHOICE PERFECTION:
GEMVARA

Gemvara, the custom jewelry company, is a great example of choice perfection. The website's design tools are so much fun to use that I have many friends who've spent hours designing Valentine's Day and Mother's Day gifts on the site. But Matt Lauzon, the company's founder and CEO, said that when he first launched the company in 2007, he didn't get it right straight out of the gate. "We made a few really bad assumptions," Lauzon said. "We thought if we made it easy for people to design their own jewelry they'd do it. But the act of customizing was unbelievably overwhelming."

Matt realized that he needed to limit choices every step of the way and provide helpful hints for consumers on what to choose, like providing a user-friendly chart of which birthstones correlate to which birth months. In order to make the design process easier, Matt also commissions professional jewelers to design beautiful pieces for customers to use as starting points, and then customers get to add their own touches—like choosing the types of gems, engraving, chain length and metal variety. "Customize" is an optional button for every design.

These starting designs are so lovely, in fact, that right now only around 30 percent of the jewelry Gemvara sells actually is customized. One hundred percent of it is made-to-order and could be customized for no extra charge, but consumers often want it just the way it is. Matt anticipates that number will rise significantly, as customers become more comfortable with customization and realize how easy it is. Right now, said Matt, "Don't assume that people want to customize. What people want is a great shopping experience."

Matt's mastery of the art of choice has certainly paid off for the bottom line. When I spoke to Matt, he told me that the company (which is private and doesn't routinely reveal its financial data) was on track to triple its sales compared to 2011, and make $25.5 million in sales during 2012. Customers spend an average of $1,000 per order; when customers come back for a second time, the average amount they spend doubles.[8]

CHAPTER 5

Made in the YOU.S.A.
Why Customizers Manufacture in America (or Wherever Their Customers Are)

I t's only lunchtime, and already more than 50,000 T-shirts, sweatshirts, hats and other consumer products have rolled off conveyor belts at this bustling factory. If you had to guess, you'd probably assume I'm writing about a concrete building somewhere in China or Latin America. But these gleaming goods aren't sitting on a factory floor in some far-flung locale. Rather, this 120,000-square-foot factory is *right here in sunny California* and is staffed by 1,000 well-paid American workers.

Welcome to Zazzle—a dazzling icon of successful 21st century *American* manufacturing. The company, which launched online in 2005, makes a lot of the same things that mass-production mainstays like Gap and Target make . . . but with one huge catch. While Zazzle sources a lot of its blank materials (like plain white T-shirts and blank ceramic mugs) from China and Latin America, the vast majority of its production takes place here in the United States. Roughly *90 percent* of the end value of all the company's products is created in the USA. In other words, it is California where the blank $2 T-shirt turns into a $20 graphic tee.

And the reason for that is simple: Zazzle is one of the world's leading customization companies. This means that every item it produces—from clothing and accessories to water bottles, postage stamps and skateboards—is customized by the buyer and made-to-order in tiny batches, often as small as just one. As a result, production has to take place close to its customers to keep delivery times fast and delivery costs low. Because its main manufacturing facility is in the United States, the company is able to produce every custom order within 24 hours of the customer clicking BUY, and goods arrive at buyers' doorsteps as fast as overnight.

Robert Beaver first conceived of the idea for the Silicon Valley company with his two sons, Bobby and Jeff, when the brothers were studying at Stanford in 1999. And since its official inception in 2005, Zazzle has systematically proved the old wisdom wrong. It turns out that successful customizing companies *should* do their manufacturing in the United States. The company's products have mostly been "Made in America" since the beginning, and it has been profitable since its very first year.

By 2008, *Business Insider* put an estimated value on the company of a quarter of a billion dollars. Zazzle is privately held and doesn't reveal its financial figures, but Bobby and Jeff told me they pulled in more than $100 million in revenue in 2011, with eight-digit profits and as many as 24 million visitors per month.

I first met Bobby and Jeff when we had all been invited to speak at a customization conference at UC Berkeley. As soon as we shook hands, I couldn't help but talk shop with them. Why don't they outsource more? Jeff, who is Zazzle's head of product and, at age 30, a year younger than Bobby, didn't miss a beat. "We actually see it as a competitive advantage to produce at home, [to] be close to our producers and deliver fast," he said.

Zazzle is a big deal for the "Made in America" label politically too. When New York City Mayor Michael Bloomberg was on the campaign trail with California gubernatorial candidate Meg Whitman in 2010, they made Zazzle's headquarters a stop on their trip. On the visit, Bloomberg applauded the company, saying, "Zazzle is a great example of the kind of innovative companies that thrive during the national recession."[1]

Zazzle is far from alone. In fact, the vast majority of successful customizers I spoke to for this book do the vast majority of their production (at least in terms of their products' end value) at home in the United States. One more great example? Shutterfly. The custom photo gift company does most of its manufacturing at state-of-the-art production facilities in North Carolina, Arizona and California that together employ nearly 1,000 Americans. "We buy our equipment and ink from U.S. companies," said Shutterfly CEO Jeffrey Housenbold, "and we've printed every single one of the more than 14 million photo books we've made here in America."

■The Future of U.S. Manufacturing

To understand exactly how much promise customizing companies have for bringing production back to America, there's no one better to talk to than Bob Marino, the CEO of custom-everything company CafePress, which pulled in $175 million in revenue in 2011. The company's U.S.-made credentials couldn't be stronger: CafePress has a 150,000-square-foot factory in Louisville, Ky. (strategically located next door to the primary UPS shipping hub), which employs more than 400 American workers. And Bob doesn't just think the U.S. production model is good for his company. In fact, he believes the custom revolution will be no less than *the way the U.S. manufacturing world reinvents itself.*" Bob told me, "You can't possibly save enough in labor to offset the shipping costs to get it to the other side of the world [so outsourcing production is] not cheaper, it is not faster, and since America is the best, it's not better."

The custom revolution will be no less than *the way the U.S. manufacturing world reinvents itself.*"

—Bob Marino, CEO of CafePress

Photo courtesy of CafePress

Figure 5.1   CAFEPRESS' CUSTOMIZING FACTORY IN KENTUCKY

The latest research suggests that Bob's prediction is going to prove incredibly prescient. As consumers come to expect greater levels of customization in everything they purchase, companies are increasingly seeing geographic proximity to their consumers as a serious competitive advantage. This is especially true as wages are rising rapidly in many of the countries America uses for outsourcing. (For example, pay for factory workers in China climbed by 69 percent between 2005 and 2010[2].) Companies that are closer to their customers can instantly respond to changes in demand and deliver customized goods without incurring sky-high shipping costs. Indeed, a 2012 poll by the Boston Consulting Group (BCG) of more than 100 companies with annual sales greater than $1 billion found that 37 percent are either planning to bring their manufacturing back home to America or are "actively considering it." That rate rose to nearly half for companies with $10 billion or more in revenues.[3] In a related report, BCG

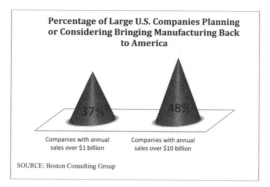

Figure 5.2   AMERICAN MANUFACTURING

predicted that such "reshoring" will add two to three million jobs to the American economy by 2020.[4]

■Save on Taxes

In addition to making fast, high-quality custom production and speedy shipments possible, doing production at home has the added benefit of cutting company taxes. In the United States, for example, the federal government charges a 17.8 percent duty on finished goods imported from other countries, but only 7 percent on unfinished goods. As a result of this and, of course, the shipping costs and time savings, even foreign customizers often open U.S. production facilities when they start targeting U.S. consumers. Spreadshirt, a German clothing customizer, produces more than 15,000 customized products every week in the company's Greensburg, Pa., production facility. Spreadshirt's success is obvious in the numbers: In mid-2011 the company celebrated its millionth order and reportedly brought in $42 million in revenue in 2010.[5]

Improvements in technology promise to bring an even greater percentage of production back home in the near future. While right now the norm for most customizers is to get blank products from the developing world, as increasingly advanced manufacturing machines are invented, the creation even of the blank object will be happening at home. One of my favorite examples of this is Case-Mate, a company that makes high-quality custom iPhone cases. Right now, Case-Mate outsources the production of the blank cases to China and does the customization of the cases in the United States (like many of the companies mentioned earlier). However, Marty Gareau, one of Case-Mate's directors, told us that he is planning to start making the blank cases in the United States soon. The cases are made using injection molding, and Marty said that the company is now big enough to get a piece of equipment capable of doing that in its U.S. production facility. In the near future, Marty told us, "We'll be totally 'Made in America,' *and* it will be cheaper [because we will completely] eliminate [overseas] shipping costs and import duties."

For more information about the companies discussed throughout this book, visit CustomNation.com/Companies.

CASE STUDY: THE BATTLE BETWEEN ZARA AND GAP

While clothing and developing-world mass production have been almost synonymous for decades, in the last several years a new paradigm has taken over. The hands-down best example of this can be seen in the battle between the world's two largest clothing retailers, Inditex Group and Gap Inc. In 2008 Inditex, the Spanish group behind clothing giant Zara, overtook America's Gap Inc., whose largest brand is the Gap store, as the largest fashion retailer in the world. The secret to its success? Customization, of course.[6]

Gap, like the other major 20th century players in clothing, makes its money by mass-producing relatively inexpensive fashion lines *before* the start of every season in cheap foreign manufacturing hubs. This method worked for Gap in the 1990s. CEO Mickey Drexler had an impressive sense of what styles would sell for the upcoming season, months before they would appear in stores. Because consumers had few affordable choices outside of this paradigm of one-style-fits-all, Drexler's good sense of trends kept shoppers coming.[7]

CONTINUES

But then Zara exploded onto the international scene with a game-changing business model. In 2001, Zara parent group Inditex launched its first IPO, which raised $2 billion in cash proceeds for the company. Following this payout, Inditex invested heavily in expanding Zara internationally.[8] This new global player couldn't have been more different from the incumbent Gap. Instead of outsourcing production to the developing world, Zara did more than 50 percent of its production in-house *at home in Spain*. By keeping control of its production and doing it at home, Zara could launch new fashion lines not in the months it took Gap but in just 10 *days*. So instead of guessing what consumers would want to wear months before the start of a season, Zara did the previously unthinkable: It asked its customers to be the designers.

Go into any Zara store today and you can see this futuristic business model in action, which the company accomplishes by mixing low-tech customer feedback with high-tech equipment (like personal digital assistants and smart cash registers). Zara's store managers engage customers in conversations to find out what designs they would like to see on the shelves. Using existing fashion lines as bases, Zara managers will ask customers if they'd like to see longer skirts, different colors, dresses with rounded necklines, work suits of different materials and a million other questions. Then they upload all these answers onto their PDAs. The managers also gather data on what customers actually want by digging through the piles of clothes that customers tried on but didn't buy—looking to find what materials, colors and styles just aren't doing it for buyers. Meanwhile, the stores' futuristic cash registers automatically tally which styles are selling the best and rank them, sending regular reports to the managers' PDAs.

In real time, Zara's managers send all this data collated on their PDAs to the Zara headquarters in La Coruna, Spain, where hundreds of designers turn the customers' ideas and desires into reality. While Zara's business model isn't "true customization" (when an individual customer logs a unique purchase that is made-to-order), it is what I like to call "customization lite," a type of customization often known in the business world as "crowdsourcing," "open-innovation" or "cocreation."

CONTINUES

Zara doesn't make its clothes to order on an individual basis. It makes them to order on a group basis, turning out thousands more styles than Gap with designs that aren't assembled in faraway places with lengthy shipping times but rather in the same country, where shipping times are measured in days instead of months. In practice, this meant that in 2008, Zara was putting out a phenomenal 30,000 totally different items in shops every year, around *10 times more* than Gap.[9]

Zara's decision to customize its fashion for its customers, and produce at home, paid off. The company's size skyrocketed from $2.43 billion in 2001 to $13.6 billion in 2007. Meanwhile, Gap started flailing. In 2003 Gap founder and chairman Dan Fisher told *Fortune* magazine, "It took us 30 years to get to $1 billion in profits and two years to get to nothing."[10] By the end of 2008, Inditex had eclipsed Gap as the largest fashion retailer in the world.

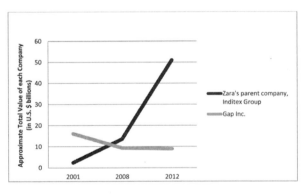

Figure 5.3   ZARA OVERTAKES GAP

The, er, gap between Gap and Zara has only grown wider since, as Zara has been able to use its penchant for customization to launch a global retail website that provides a customized shopping experience. On Zara's website, which launched in 2010, shoppers can customize the virtual aisles they browse in detail. In the dresses section, for example, a shopper can effectively create a custom aisle by choosing *characteristics* (from mini to evening), *color* (from camel to ecru), *size* (from XXS to XXL) and *price* (from under $10 to more than $70). In practice, the customer gets the same experience she would get

CONTINUES

CONTINUED

walking into a high-end boutique and asking the trusted salesperson for a recommendation. "I'm looking for a red mini dress for less than $60 in a size small," says the shopper. And the website answers immediately, with a glossy photograph of—to cite an example from the spring 2012—the Evassee Jersey Dress.

That contrasts sharply with Gap's website, which only offers shoppers the ability to customize the choices of product that appear under dresses by size. Consumers now expect more. They want their shopping experiences to feel customized. The proof is all in the numbers. In 2010, the year the Zara website launched, Gap Inc.'s net income rose by just 9 percent. At the same time, Inditex Group, Zara's parent company, saw its net income skyrocket by 32 percent.

CHAPTER 6

The Future of Commerce
Customize Everything, Everywhere, All the Time

Imagine you need a new pair of jeans. You go online to your favorite store and browse the styles it offers. You settle on a pair of cool 1970s retro flares and click TRY ON. But here's the weird part: You don't have to put in your size, wait until they're delivered to try them on or worry if they'll fit.

Instead, the TRY ON button takes you to a screen that reads "Stand Up While We Take Your Measurements." You stand up and hold a standard-sized product (like a ballpoint pen or a credit card) against the top of your waistline. Your computer's camera then takes a photo of your bottom half from four different angles while you turn around once in order to enable it to photograph your front, back and two sides. Based on this information, the software program on the store's website automatically calculates all your real-life measurements instantaneously and creates the sewing pattern necessary to make the flare jeans you chose made-to-measure and tailor-perfect for you.

The program then virtually creates a mock-up of these precise jeans and juxtaposes them on the picture your computer just took of you. In real-time, and without ever having to disrobe, you see real photographs of you wearing these custom-fit flare jeans from four different angles. Don't like the color? Just change it with the click of a button. Want to add a print? Another single click. Using your mouse (or finger, if your screen is touch-based), you'll be able to move, add or resize pockets, buttons and other embellishments. When you settle on the perfect look, you can click BUY and they'll be made-to-order within 24 hours and arrive at your door within the week.

This kind of technology might sound like something out of a science-fiction movie, but there are dozens of companies that have already developed working pieces of it. Chic custom-clothing companies, including Made to Fit Me, Proper Cloth, ShirtsMyWay, Blank Label and unitedstyles, allow customers to design everything from tailored shirts and suits to silk dresses and trendy skirts, and then create the pieces to order exactly to fit their clients' own measurements (which clients take themselves at home). Best of all, these totally customized pieces cost roughly the same as you'd pay for off-the-rack items in a department store. There are also some companies that have started using consumers' own photographs in the design process. Design Your Own Eyewear, for instance, asks users to upload photos of themselves. Then customers can superimpose different glasses over their own images and digitally stretch or alter the frames to suit their own faces.

The possibilities of such software extend way past fashion. Zazzle promises a near-future in which we will be able to custom design every object in our entire homes, tailor-made to fit our homes' precise measurements. In November 2011, Zazzle cofounder Bobby Beaver launched the first piece of this future, which the company calls "In Situ." Customers can now go to Zazzle's enormous, and totally customizable, wall art section and see what a given piece would look like in their own home, made-to-measure for the exact wall they want to hang it on, without ever having to get out a tape measure.

Here's how it works: You go on Zazzle and choose a wall print you love—say a 16th century map of the world. Then click SEE ON YOUR WALL!

Zazzle asks you to print out a black-and-white "marker" on your standard printer. This marker is basically just a stylized "Z" printed on standard letter-sized paper, which gives Zazzle's software a starting point to take your wall's measurements. Stick this paper on whatever wall you want with tape, take a picture with your camera and upload the photo to Zazzle. Zazzle takes care of the rest. It automatically measures the wall, using the marker as its guide and then superimposes the print you'd like on that wall, complete with realistic lighting from your own home environment. Within 10 minutes, you're looking at a photograph of your own wall with the print you're considering buying *on* it.

Bobby imagines that eventually Zazzle's software will allow you to stand in an empty room in a new house you've just bought and fill it from scratch with incredible furniture, carpets and art from all over the world—testing different combinations, trying various colors, customizing *everything*—and only buying when you've already seen a lighting-perfect mock-up of what your actual room will look like with everything in place. If this sounds like a futuristic, space-age virtual reality, you'd be right. Bobby's IT team is ahead of the curve. Indeed, one of Zazzle's head Web design engineers actually created one of the world's first-ever virtual reality systems for NASA back in the early 1980s. "Our focus is on 10 years from now," Bobby told us. "This is just the beginning."

And where is the end? Well, if you ask Bobby and his brother and Zazzle cofounder Jeff, they will tell you, "We think there is space for a new Amazon." This new Amazon would have everything the current Amazon has (cars, shoes, bags, shirts, DVDs, furniture, etc.) with one big difference: Everything it sold would be customizable.

"I believe the future of *all* commerce is customization," Jeff told me.

Th[e] new Amazon would have everything the current Amazon has (cars, shoes, bags, shirts, DVDs, furniture, etc.) with one big difference: Everything it sold would be customizable.

I believe that by the time my nephews, who are three and four years old right now, are my age, they'll think about how I grew up in an age where my clothes only fit well-enough, my store-bought foods had ingredients I didn't like and I had to settle for the limited selection of, well, everything—and they'll find it positively archaic. I already see signs of it in my nephews' evolving tastes. Riley, who is four, was eating a store-bought nutrition bar the other day (his mom had run out of YouBars) and balked, saying, "Mommy, I hate these raisins. Why didn't you tell them *not* to put any in?"

■ Digital Manufacturing

The remaining question, of course, is how will machines make all these different types of custom goods for anything near the price that they currently mass produce the same type of goods? In chapters one and two, I discussed two of the key technological developments that have happened since 2000 to make this possible: One, for the first time in history, the internet connected producers directly to consumers, without the need for brick-and-mortar retailers; and two, online design tools gave consumers the physical ability to design their own goods, from jewelry to business cards, without expensive expert help.

But there is also a futuristic third part that is just developing now. Mass production dominated the 20th century largely thanks to assembly lines, which are great at mass producing millions of identical products but terrible at customizing. But in this new age of digital information, assembly lines are starting to be replaced by a brand-new type of machine: 3-D printers.

Say what? Well, as the name suggests, 3-D printers link up to computers just like regular old 2-D printers do. The revolutionary thing? Instead of dripping liquid ink onto paper to create words and designs like our current printers do, 3-D printers use all sorts of materials, like liquid plastic, liquid metal and liquid glass, to create real 3-D objects from digital blueprints. Instead of cutting, bending and splicing materials like the typical machines on assembly lines do, 3-D printers make things from the bottom up by depositing material, layer by layer. These printers literally print out *stuff* (vases, globes, bicycles—anything you can imagine) by dripping liquid material down onto a "creation tray." In the case of objects made of multiple materials, like bicycles' metal frames and leather seats, different materials are added from different cartridges, just like standard color printers can use a rainbow of different colors and not just black.

This type of production (called "additive manufacturing" because material is "added" from the bottom up) makes it just as cheap to create a million completely customized bicycles as a million identical ones, much in the same way that a regular printer can print a million different letters for roughly the same price and ease that it can print the same single letter a million times. Traditionally, machines have been terrible at making custom goods. However, 3-D printers are the revolutionary machines that promise to change that for good.

These 3-D printers aren't yet good enough to make a laptop or an airplane, but they *are* being used to make special parts for certain airplanes and custom covers for laptops. The technology is new, but products from 3-D printers are already so widespread that it's likely you've come into contact with them without even knowing it: They make hearing aids customized for the exact shape of the user's ear, gearboxes custom-designed for racing cars and replacement hips custom-built to fit the wearer's body. On top of that, dozens of avant-garde companies, including i.materialise, Shapeways, Ponoko and Polyvore, use 3-D printers for all their standard production of unique small-run designs of goods, like business card holders and tables.[1] Additive manufacturing is so exciting that in April 2012, *The Economist* ran a cover package that hailed digital manufacturing as the "Third Industrial Revolution"!

Figure 6.1   MAKERBOT INDUSTRIES' "REPLICATOR"
Source: Photo Courtesy of Makerbot® Industries, LLC

This 3-D printer, which came to market in early 2012, is one of the most affordable high-quality 3-D printers currently available. It can create objects up to 9x6x6 inches in size in a variety of colors and plastics and costs $1,750.

Academics are equally enthralled. At UC Berkeley's Mass Customization conference in 2011, an entire afternoon was dedicated to 3-D printing. And Cornell University has an extensive research project called Fab@ Home, which makes, develops and shares the hardware and software designs for 3-D printers. Jeff Lipton, the head of Fab@Home, told us that he believes 3-D printers will be mainstream in the next decade and that they'll completely revolutionize the way we live. "The possibilities are limitless," he said. "We can't even know how exactly they will change our lives yet. It would be like asking someone in the 1970s to guess how the internet would change our lives. It's going to change absolutely everything."

"The possibilities are limitless....We can't even know how exactly [3-D printers] will change our lives yet. It would be like asking someone in the 1970s to guess how the internet would change our lives."

—Jeff Lipton, head of Fab@Home

These 3-D printers won't just print objects like bicycles, toy cars and hearing aids; they'll also be available in different versions to sew clothes and make food. Going back to the flare jeans, for example, companies will be able to create your completely custom jeans for the same price as a mass-produced pair thanks to 3-D printers that create clothes. The food versions of 3-D printers are equally exciting. Right now, one of the coolest ways they're being used is at high-end bakeries to "print" wedding cakes with the couples' names written in cursive icing inside every slice, and at The Culinary Institute of America in New York, where they make things like rocket ship–shaped scallops.[2]

Best of all, with 3-D printers, anytime that anyone comes up with a great object that solves an existing problem, the inventor will be able to disseminate the new invention with unbelievable speed. If a design student in Thailand invents a clothing hanger that makes it impossible for clothes to slip off, she'd be able to distribute the blueprint for her invention to the world like an iPhone app, and small companies with 3-D printers could create them for consumers that same day.

Consumers would be able to print those hangers in whatever color or material they want and even have their own name or phrase emblazoned on the side of each one, simply for the cost of the blueprint and the additive manufacturing printout. The sewing pattern for the custom jeans that we talked about at the beginning of this chapter will be as likely to come from a loved-by-all-your-friends-on-Facebook trendsetting 17-year-old fashion student in Dubai as it is to come from the Gap. And the factory of the future won't be the mass-production plant in the developing world; it will much more likely be your tech-savvy neighbor's garage … or anywhere you can rent the use of a 3-D printer.

In the same way that the invention of the printing press in the middle of the last millennium democratized knowledge by making it possible for people outside of the elite to get books, 3-D printers promise to democratize innovation for this millennium. It will no longer simply be the connected, corporate-funded elite who will be able to create inventions and designs that reach the masses. In the 21st century, everyone will have the tools necessary to create and spread their creations. Small audiences, even as small as one, will have a voice to ask for a custom product to meet their needs, and individuals will have the power to answer.

In the same way that the invention of the printing press in the middle of the last millennium democratized knowledge by making it possible for people outside of the elite to get books, 3-D printers promise to democratize innovation for this millennium.

Not Just Online and at Home, but Everywhere, All the Time

At first glance, the description of the custom-everything future might seem like an isolating place, full of people living their lives from home computer-based virtual reality systems. But in *real* reality, a custom nation fosters meaningful connections more than ever before. When you go shopping online, you'll be online with dozens of your friends at the same time, showing all of them the picture of you in the new jeans to see if they like them. And when you go to real shopping malls, the staff will be more interested in getting to know you—and really help you—than ever before. You'll be able to customize any of the things you find with the click of a finger from their in-store touch screens. Clothing stores will have measurement stations instead of dressing rooms. When you decide to buy, you could buy something off-the-rack or get it customized in the store to be printed that day at the company's 3-D printer production facility (and delivered to your home that day).

Best of all, because you'll be able to easily buy whatever you want online, brick-and-mortar stores will start having loftier goals than simply sales. They'll become places where events happen, you learn things and you get to know people. If this seems unlikely, there is already one hugely successful brand that embodies this futuristic model of store for experience's sake: Apple. If you look in any Apple store, you'll see the difference immediately. It's more like a place-to-be than a place-to-buy. Part techie-playground, part computer problem–solving mecca, Apple doesn't feel like it's trying to sell you anything when you go in. Rather, it's teaching you about the brand and providing excellent customer service to keep you as a loyal customer. Customers are invited to come in, hang out and—literally—*play* with all the iMacs, iPads and iPhones on display. In the large stores, there's usually even a section for kids to play video games on Apple products.

Perhaps most important of all, the people who work there are actually helpful, and you get to know them as members of the community. The pinnacle of this is the excellently named Genius Bar at the back of some stores, which is full of Apple whizzes who can answer questions or provide hands-on technical support for any Apple product you already own. One extremely friendly, very knowledgeable Genius whom Emily met at an Apple store at a mall in Connecticut told her that he has to hide his identity sometimes, "If I have to get somewhere fast when I'm in this mall, I have to wear a hat. People recognize me and will stop me to ask me all sorts of tech questions. It's like being a mini-celebrity."

Quieter, Greener, Kinder, More Relevant

The custom-everything future will also eliminate one of the most common complaints people have about the modern world: information overload. When the internet came along, our old filters for information—the top TV news programs and our local newspapers—disappeared and were replaced by a million different newspapers, news stations and blogs available online, and the process of figuring out what matters became exhausting. Companies specializing in making customized recommendations based on what you already like are fixing this problem . . . and they're getting better and better at it.

The giant early pioneer in this was Amazon, which recommends everything from books to dog leashes by deducing what you would "also like" based on what you have previously bought. Dozens of other companies now do this for dozens of other commodities. Pandora does it for music. Netflix does it for movies and television shows.[3] Ness, an iPhone app, does it for restaurant recommendations. And, perhaps most promising of all for the noninformation-overload future, there's Hunch, which has the ambitious goal of creating a complete "taste graph" of the Web. Hunch's ultimate aim would be to be able to tell you what you'd enjoy in almost everything—clubs, parties, events, books, magazines, shoes, games and orange juice—simply based on the information you already have online, like your Facebook profile and previous Google searches.

Going hand-in-hand with information overload, we are also—as a society—combating *stuff* overload. And this is, perhaps, the very best thing the custom business model has to offer. In the custom world, nothing is made unless it is wanted, and so it will drastically cut waste. We could be close to an era where no more unsold inventory ever gets carted off to landfills. What's more, with 3-D printers, everything we buy will be produced much closer to home, at in-country factories, so there won't be any carbon dioxide polluting the atmosphere as commodities fly around the globe getting from where they're made to where they're used.

In the custom world, nothing is made unless it is wanted, and so it will drastically cut waste.

To me, though—probably because I work in the food industry and spend a lot of time thinking about food—the pinnacle of customization is in the realm of eating. The new world of customization holds the potential to create not just perfect custom diets for each of us as individuals, but also the perfect custom diet for each society as a whole. Consider these two statistics: 1) In the United States today, we throw away approximately 25 percent of the food we buy, in the form of spoilage in overstocked refrigerators and uneaten leftovers.[4] 2) At the same time, the number of people in America struggling to put adequate food on their tables is at an all-time high. According to a study by the U.S. Department of Agriculture, 50 million people in the United States, including nearly 17 million children, struggle to get enough to eat or suffer from malnourishment.[5]

In the not-too-distant future, I believe the technology of customization could be harnessed to tell us when we have food in our refrigerators that is about to spoil and how close the nearest table that needs it is. It could be just around the corner.

This revolution will be edible.

For more information about the companies discussed throughout this book, visit CustomNation.com/Companies.

section 2

BECOME THE NEXT GREAT CUSTOMIZER

CHAPTER

Launching Your New CIY Business

o you have a business idea? Well, in the new world of customization, you can stop daydreaming and do it. Back in the 20th century, launching a new business was an expensive, risky undertaking. You had to have up-front financing to pay for production, a costly brick-and-mortar storefront (or, at least, shelf space in one) and a highly paid staff.

Now all it takes to set up shop is a great product or service and a website. Whatever your basic idea for a business, making it customized is the easiest and best way to turn it from general concept into viable, profitable reality. When you sell a made-to-order product, you get paid *before* you make anything, so your monetary risk can be close to nothing. Plus, with customers contributing their own ideas and excitement for free, your design-related labor costs and marketing expenses will be much lower than in traditional mass-production businesses.

■ Dell Inc.

The most iconic (and oldest) example of the cost-effectiveness of starting a custom business comes from Michael Dell. In 1984, he launched Dell Inc.

from his college dorm room with just $1,000. His business model of making computers to order meant he didn't need any more up-front financing than that tiny sum. But his lean start didn't prevent lightning-speed success: By 1992, Michael was the youngest CEO of a Fortune 500 company.

If you're reading this, it's likely that you too have always had an entrepreneurial dream—maybe to run a trendy ice cream parlor, launch a wine label or create designer purses. Many of us spend years daydreaming about these ideas while sitting in our cubicles at 9-to-5 jobs we can barely stand. In all likelihood, the only reason you haven't actually launched your business is because you believe you can't—perhaps because you lack the funds, knowledge or experience to do so.

Here are the top concerns that would-be entrepreneurs typically harbor:

◆ You don't think you have enough funding to get it off the ground.
◆ You don't know where you would sell your product, or how you would get customers.
◆ You don't want to quit your job until you have established that you can make money with your new venture.

Well, I can tell you how to overcome all of these concerns. I've come up with seven straightforward steps that you can use to launch a new customizing business for as little as $1,000 without quitting your day job. But first, here's the exciting story of one entrepreneur who shows just how possible it is.

■ Practically Risk-Free: Case Study of a Classic CIY Startup

Jan-Christoph Goetze isn't your typical risk-taking entrepreneur. With his curly white hair, rosy face and infectious smile, you'd be more inclined to guess that he's something like an architect. And that's what Jan-Christoph used to be. The German Cornell graduate, who moved to the United States to take a job at one of the country's leading architecture firms in the late 1990s, thought he would keep working long hours designing buildings until he retired at a ripe old age. But he wasn't happy with the long hours, or being so far from home. Jan-Christoph used to spend his weekends browsing the aisles of bookshops and daydreaming.

"When you're growing up, you dream that you are the hero in James Bond," he told me when we met. "I thought it would be incredible to give people—both children and adults—the ability to actually become the stars of novels."

So in 2003, Jan-Christoph quit his job as an architect and moved back to Germany to launch a business to do exactly that. "I didn't need to quit my job to do it," he said, "but I was sick of working overtime and wanted to come home to Germany."

With just 5,000 euros (roughly $6,300) and a passion for the printed word, Jan-Christoph created PersonalNOVEL, a company that allows customers to personalize novels and children's books, making the stories about themselves. Jan-Christoph turns his clients into fictional heroes by using his interactive but fairly simple website to take down clients' details, like their names, the names of the people they love, and their hair and eye color. The results are as enchanting as any happily ever after. Parents can give their kids stories that star them as pirates or princesses, women can give their husbands romance novels starring the two of them as passionate lovers and men can write their "dream autobiographies," starring themselves as James Bond-esque spies.

Jan-Christoph's business model is about as dream-inspired as it gets, but by selling customization and outsourcing production to a local high-quality printer, all he needed in order to launch was a website and a sense of creativity. He didn't need to buy any material—not even a piece of paper—before making his first sale, so his risk was low. And the speed of seeing results was breakneck: He launched in September 2003, and his company was profitable by that December.

The number of sales Jan-Christoph has made since then is even more astounding. The onetime architect has sold more than 200,000 books for between 25 euros (for paperback) and 50 euros (for hardcover) each. Every single year, PersonalNOVEL has enjoyed growth of between 10 percent and 20 percent, thanks simply to word-of-mouth recommendations, targeted online advertising and some glowing reviews in women's magazines, including *Glamour*, *Cosmopolitan*, and *Elle*. Without any outside investment, he has organically grown the business to a bustling 15 full-time employees, including three who do nothing but customer service, and has commissioned more than 50 authors to write books that lend themselves to personalization. In total, PersonalNOVEL's customers can now choose from 250 different original titles.

Breaking It Down—Seven Straightforward Steps to Launching a Successful Custom Business

Step 1: Choose Your Business

My coauthor, Emily, has interviewed some of the most successful and well-known entrepreneurs in the world, including Virgin's CEO and founder Richard Branson and The Body Shop's late founder Anita Roddick, and one of the top tips that all the most enviable entrepreneurs give is: Have fun!

I couldn't agree more. Starting a new business involves a large commitment of time and energy. Before I actually launched YouBar, I was spending nearly every waking hour thinking about my new business and strategizing my business plan (even while doing other things), and almost everyone I know who is a successful entrepreneur has a similar story. Unless you love your business, you won't enjoy working on it for the number of hours required. The Body Shop's Roddick summed up the successful entrepreneur's relationship with work well when she said, "I have no idea what work is anymore. It is so much a part of my life."[1]

The moral? Whatever business you've been dreaming about is the one you should launch.

"I have no idea what work is anymore. It is so much a part of my life."

—Anita Roddick, founder of The Body Shop

CUSTOM INTERNSHIP

What if you want to work in an industry that you don't have any experience in? Get a custom internship. Soon after launching YouBar, when my mom and I were still hand-making every single bar ourselves, we realized that it would be essential to get experience working for an existing custom food company. All of my previous jobs and internships had been in offices; I had no experience in a commercial kitchen, much less a customizing kitchen. The problem was that there was no such thing as a custom nutrition bar company because, well, YouBar was the first. This was a good thing from a marketing perspective, but for firsthand kitchen knowledge I needed something similar. My mom and I thought hard about how to get that necessary experience and came up with Jamba Juice, the fast-service smoothie restaurant that makes customized juices to order.

So, I put on my best suit and walked into a local Jamba Juice store that had a "Help Needed" sign on the door. I handed my resume, which started with my recent graduation from USC with a business degree, to the 19-year-old manager. And he looked at me, my resume and my suit with a lot of confusion. "What position are you looking for?" he asked. I replied with exactly what I thought you were supposed to say, "I want to start at the bottom and work my way up." He looked baffled and told me he'd call me. I didn't get the job.

That was definitely one of my lowest points as an entrepreneur. Here I was, trying to start my own company, and I couldn't even get a minimum wage–paying job at Jamba Juice. But I picked myself up and decided to try a different tack. I swapped my suit for shorts and flip-flops, took everything off my resume except my high school diploma and experience as a

CONTINUES

snowboard instructor, and drove across town to a different Jamba Juice that was looking for new employees. I handed the teenage manager in this store my pared-down resume, and when he asked me why I wanted to work there, I simply said, "I like juice." He gave me the job on the spot.

Working at Jamba Juice for minimum wage wasn't the most glamorous thing I've done as an entrepreneur. In fact, it was often extremely humbling, but it was one of the most important things I did in those early months. While working at Jamba Juice, I learned an enormous amount about what makes a commercial kitchen tick day in and day out: what makes a good manager, how to train staff, how to keep people motivated, how to store fresh ingredients, what the proper protocols are for cleaning a kitchen, how to wash the equipment, how to keep track of inventory and what makes good (and bad) customer service.

My advice would be that if you're going into an industry you haven't had previous experience in, it's invaluable to get an unpaid internship, or as in my case, a low-paying job in that industry. While it will almost certainly pay less than what your time is worth, if it pays at all, the ultimate value to your new company will be enormous.

Step 2: Set Yourself Apart

The key to choosing the right business is to go with what you love, but it is also vital to set yourself apart from the ever-growing competition. Entrepreneurship is on the rise. Between the start of 2009 and the end of 2010, for example, Americans created more than 1 million new businesses.[2] Adding a custom twist to your product can often be all the originality and differentiation you'll need. Indeed, customization is such a hot trend for new businesses that *Entrepreneur* magazine named it as one of the Top Ten Trends in 2012.[3]

eCreamery Ice Cream & Gelato is an excellent example of this. Thanks simply to adding customization to the age-old business of selling ice cream, founders Abby Jordan and Becky App launched a brand-new business that attracted press attention the way kids are drawn to, well, ice cream.

Abby and Becky's story started in the early 2000s. At the time, the two women were working together in the marketing department of a luxury jewelry store that specialized in personalized gifts. During long lunches, they would often wonder, "How could this business model get any better?" Their "aha" moment came when they had the idea to sell "*edible* customized gifts"—custom ice cream. So in 2006 they purchased the domain name eCreamery.com from Rod Valeroso, a student with a family ice cream business, who had designed the website's basic layout and ran it with limited functionality for several years.

When Abby and Becky took over, they used their marketing backgrounds—and enviable ice cream creation skills—and launched the concept of custom ice cream to the world. At eCreamery, Becky and Abby now invite their customers to design their own flavors of ice cream online. The company's in-house chefs then turn these creations into reality and ship them anywhere in the United States at a delectable 10 degrees below zero, complete with personalized packaging.

Thanks to their business plan's, ahem, utter originality, eCreamery was an overnight success. Within a week of launching in 2007, eCreamery's unique product was picked up by the Food Network. Since then, the company's custom ice cream has been featured everywhere from *The New York Times* to the *Today* show. Celebrity chef Rachael Ray is a huge fan, and Becky and Abby have shipped orders to special events across the country, including one at the White House. By 2010 (three years after launching), eCreamery.com was pulling in more than half a million dollars in annual sales. In 2011, even amid the recession, eCreamery's sales were up by 40 percent. "People have an emotional connection with ice cream," Becky said. "We've made the experience of creating the flavor as fun as it is eating it."

As eCreamery illustrates, customization itself is often enough to turn a stale, age-old business idea (selling ice cream is hardly original) into a delicious new fresh one. However, it's important to keep in mind that in the past five years, customization has already started taking off in several key industries, so avoiding those is important if you want to benefit from the originality of customization.

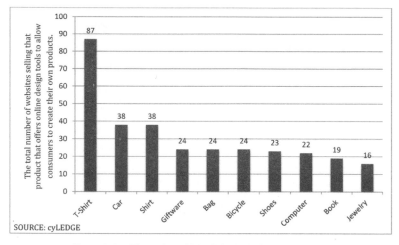

Figure 7.1 TOP 10 CATEGORIES OF CUSTOMIZED GOODS

The sectors on this chart indicate where you have to use the most caution launching a new custom business to avoid replicating something that already exists and losing the greatest potential of free press as a result. Just because there are already nearly 100 T-shirt customizers, that doesn't mean you can't go into it. You just need to make sure you add an original twist, like making custom baby T-shirts using organic cotton.

For the most up-to-date list of customizers working in your desired field, go to the Custom Nation website, CustomNation.com, to find the "Company Customizer." Then enter the type of company you're planning to launch, and the Company Customizer will produce a printable sheet of information, including the names of other custom companies operating in that category of goods.

Step 3: Determine Your Target Market

Entrepreneurs naturally think big, and that's usually a good thing. But when it comes to the first steps of starting a new business, giant ambitions can be a hindrance to getting started. When I talk to people who would like to start a new company, their business models often rely on what I call the "one million quarters" plan.

Take, for example, the acquaintance of mine—let's call her Erica— who wanted to launch a freshly baked custom cupcake company. Her idea was that customers would place an order, and their cupcakes (with their own choice of base cake flavor, colorful frosting and topping decorations) would be baked to order and delivered to their doors. The problem was that with such a high-labor business and such a relatively inexpensive product, her profit margins were going to be tight.

"It's okay," she told me. "Everyone loves cupcakes, and there are 10 million people in Los Angeles. Even if I only get a tenth of those people to buy cupcakes, and I'm making a quarter from each one, I'll have a quarter of a million dollars in profits the first year!"

Unsurprisingly, Erica never launched the business. Her target market was too unfocused. A million quarters has a nice ring to it as a cocktail party sound bite, but contemplating the reality of getting that number of customers is pretty scary when most of us only have a couple hundred real-life contacts through friends, clubs, social networks, online communities, schools, religious organizations and the like.

Interestingly, those couple hundred genuine contacts can be the key to success. Instead of starting with the idea of needing a million sales, start with needing just 50. Going back to Erica, for example, she already had around 50 people who had tried her cupcakes at her own siblings' birthday parties, had loved them and had told her that they would be early customers. Fifty sales wouldn't be enough to quit her job, but if Erica had planned her production method and hours carefully (see Step 4), she could have used those 50 guaranteed early sales to launch her company (while still keeping her day job), get buzz about it going online and start figuring out what genre of customer would be her first target market, a base from which she could then expand. For Erica, the early interest she already had from the parents of her younger siblings' friends could have indicated to her that targeting that demographic first would make sense: parents of grade-school–age children looking for delicious custom cupcake birthday cakes for their own kids' parties.

At YouBar, our first target customers were fitness enthusiasts. We saw our custom bars as having great value for people such as athletes who needed specific combinations of foods, detailed calorie counts and individually balanced nutrients (protein, carbs, etc.). This market was also easy for us to reach using personal contacts because both my cofounder and I were snowboard instructors at the time, and I was training for my first marathon. Our friends and acquaintances through these exercise-related activities ultimately became some of our first customers.

You'll hear this story again and again from successful entrepreneurs. Tiny Prints, a card printer that offers high-quality custom birth announcements and birthday party invitations, was cofounded by Ed Han in 2004 when he was expecting his first child and had a circle of friends who were new parents. It clearly paid off: Han and the other Tiny Print owners sold the company in 2011 for $333 million.

To summarize: It is important to know exactly who your initial key target market is and ideally have a personal social circle relating to it. If you do that, then you can have a manageable, focused launch (which I will outline in detail in Step 7), instead of hoping to hook an amorphous million. As you become established and start growing, your target market will naturally expand. In our case, an early secondary market was moms trying to provide easy, healthy snacks for their children.

ADVICE FROM THE CEO OF A CUSTOMIZING COMPANY WORTH APPROXIMATELY $1 BILLION

I asked Jeffrey Housenbold from Shutterfly, the company that we profiled in chapter two, what advice he'd give an entrepreneur or business executive who wanted to get into customizing. Here's what he had to say:

Know who your customer is and build your business around that customer. Ninety-eight percent of small businesses fail because the owners treat the business as a love. What you really have to know is what your *customer* loves. You have to know what problems your customers are having in their lives, and you have to build solutions. For us, 75 percent of our customers are female, 25 to 50 years old, college educated, brand conscious and brand loyal. They don't care about technology other than how it makes life easier and faster.

[After getting to know your customer, then] you have to *differentiate, differentiate, differentiate.* We all compete with Amazon and Walmart; you really have to think about how you're offering something different and better. Be obsessive about how you're going to delight your customers. Getting a customer one time isn't enough to build a successful business today. We aim for 100 percent customer satisfaction and offer 100 percent satisfaction guaranteed. Seventy-five percent of our business is repeat business. That is a really good testament to the loyalty of our customers.

We want to build a deep personal relationship with our customers in a place where they trust us with life's memories. Howard Schultz has built a great business with coffee, even though people said it was a commodity and consumers would not pay more. iPods are not the best MP3 players, but the user experience is great. We are building a premium lifestyle brand in the vein of Starbucks or Apple.

Customizing is a great business model because it speaks to an age-old human desire. It has always been a human desire to have something unique. In the 1940s all the way

CONTINUES

CONTINUED

until the 1990s, it was a push world. Consumers had to accept mass-produced products. The technology wasn't there for them to be unique. But over time—through the advent of technology—we can now choose. I think every generation has wanted to express themselves. It goes all the way back to Egypt and hieroglyphics. The technology has changed, but the core desire to capture your time on earth and tell your story hasn't. At Shutterfly, that's our main aim: to enable our customers to tell their stories.

Figure 7.2   SHUTTERFLY
Source: Photo courtesy of Shutterfly

Step 4: Join Your Community and Secure Your Production Method

So, you've decided to become the next great T-shirt customizer, car accessory customizer or even energy bar customizer? That's wonderful! One thing you'll find out as soon as you enter the world of custom business is that, far from being competitive with each other, many owners of custom businesses actually want to help each other. Customization is still a relatively new concept on a large scale. And so, far from fighting to command slices of a fixed-size pie, customizers (even those producing the same type of products) often work together to increase consumer awareness that customization of their product is possible and *make the pie bigger*.

My personal experience supports this. Since launching YouBar, there have been several companies that have copied our business model. The first time this happened, I'll admit I was nervous that we would lose sales to competition. But it turned out that I couldn't have been more wrong. Whenever a competitor got good press, it simply increased public awareness that it was possible to get a high-quality custom bar for an affordable price tag, something that helped me as much as my competition. In short, I don't feel that I'm competing against other bar customizers as much as I believe that I'm working with them to compete against the status-quo companies making mass-produced bars that are falling short of customers' individual needs.

> I don't feel that I'm competing against other bar customizers as much as I believe that I'm working with them to compete against the status-quo companies making mass-produced bars that are falling short of customers' individual needs.

Shutterfly's Jeff Housenhold told me that he often gets asked about how he plans to steal customers from competitors like Snapfish. "The reality is that I'm not trying to steal their customers," he said. "We have less than 10 percent market penetration as an industry. I'm worried about [how to get] the other 90 percent."

The unity between seeming competitors in the world of customization can prove particularly useful when you're first starting out. If there is an existing customizer working in the field you would like to get into, it can often make sense to explore the idea of sharing production with that company, or if they are a lot bigger, outsourcing to them altogether, especially if the type of customization you offer complements the type they offer. There's no need to reinvent the wheel.

Consider, for example, the world of customized women's designer shoes, a growing share of the enormous $143 billion global market for fashion footwear. Claudia Kieserling, the CEO of selve, a German company that has been making custom women's shoes since 2000, produces her company's shoes at a factory in China that she chose because it was capable of handling single made-to-order purchases. In 2010, a brand-new women's shoe customizer came on the scene: Milk & Honey, headed

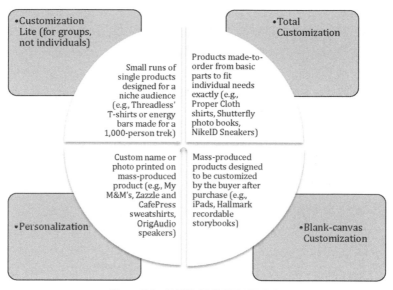

Figure 7.3 TYPES OF CUSTOMIZATION

up by Ilissa Howard, an American expat living in Hong Kong. In the normal world of retail, Claudia would have viewed Milk & Honey as a competitor. But this is customization so she didn't see it that way. In fact, Claudia actually invited Ilissa to share the Chinese production facility she had in place. "I don't know what we would have done without Claudia," Ilissa told me.

Jan-Christoph Goetze, the architect-owner of PersonalNOVEL, has a similar story. When he launched his business, he contracted a local custom publisher capable of printing high-quality, single-run books. Jan-Christoph didn't want to be a publisher, or invest the money necessary to do that; he wanted to create a specific magical custom item for consumers. In the terms of the Types of Customization chart, Jan-Christoph's publisher was the Total Customizer while PersonalNOVEL was, in effect, a Personalizer, adding individualization to books with blank portions. When

PersonalNOVEL proved so successful that Jan-Christoph could have afforded to go into publishing himself, he was so happy with the custom publisher he had used to build his business that he invested in it directly and is now a part-owner. When we asked Jan-Christoph what his top piece of advice would be to an entrepreneur who wanted to launch a custom business, he said, "Keep it simple." In other words, if you have a great idea for a product, stick to that. You don't necessarily need to overextend yourself to become a producer.

If you do want to get into production, decide whether you want to make your product from scratch or whether you want to work with partially assembled materials. Rickshaw Bagworks, a custom messenger bag company based in San Francisco, sources the "chassis," the basic black messenger bag it uses as the base for all its bags, from a mass-production factory in China. However, the company personalizes all the bags it sells at its San Francisco factory with a totally customizable front flap, customizable pockets, laptop sleeves and flaps. "That's where we create a personality for this otherwise black chassis," said founder and CEO Mark Dwight. Not only does this mean Mark doesn't have to be in the business of creating the basic product but it also means his inventory never gets outdated. "This model totally derisks the inventory," he said. "I can respond to any fashion, fad or trend just by getting the right fabric." (In terms of the Types of Customization chart, Rickshaw Bagworks walks the line between Total Customizer and Personalizer.)

Using existing customization companies for production is also a great way to launch a business that is custom-designed for a specific niche population. Say you've always dreamed of launching a trendy wine label to fit the style and tastes of your avant-garde Brooklyn neighborhood—you can do it with Crushpad. Say you've thought of an amazing design for man bags to appeal to Occupy Wall Street sympathizers—you can do it with Rickshaw Bagworks. Say you know exactly the kind of trendy dress that would sell well at your university—you can do it on unitedstyles).

At YouBar we produce medium-sized runs of energy bars (anywhere from 100 to 50,000 single-type bars) for nutritionists and dieticians around the country. These experts design their bars to fit the exact dietary specifications they and their clients subscribe to, and the bars are all wrapped in packages with these experts' self-styled and unique packaging, giving them a high-end retail product that is completely their own.

Huge examples of this custom production method come from the likes of CafePress, Zazzle and Shutterfly. These customization giants are the production facilities of literally countless startup designers making everything from wall art to T-shirts to coffee mugs for small groups of customers linked by similar aesthetic, moral or political views. Indeed, Zazzle has ambitions to indirectly employ *more than 1 million people* within the next decade by providing the production for these creative niche designers. "It seems like every day I hear another story about someone who has been able to quit his job at Walmart because he's selling so much through Zazzle," company cofounder Jeff Beaver told me. *The Wall Street Journal* has reported on individual designers making more than $1 million in revenue a year through designing topical political gear, like red and blue flip-flops, on websites that poke fun at the latest phrases coming out of politicians' mouths.

In summary: Just like customized products, customization itself comes in all shapes and sizes. When launching your company, decide which one best suits your idea (the four key types are in the Types of Customization chart, but it is possible to be a mixture of two different categories). It's likely that you'll be able to find an existing customizer who can help you get production off the ground quickly and affordably.

CRUSHPAD: LAUNCH YOUR OWN WINE LABEL WITHOUT BUYING A VINEYARD

One beautiful autumn morning in 2010, Rick Speer, a successful biologist from Chicago, was pressing grapes in Napa Valley to blend for his new wine label. Contrary to appearances, Rick isn't independently wealthy. He doesn't own a vineyard or have a part-time California residence. He's making his very own wine—a

CONTINUES

CONTINUED

batch of 25 cases, or 300 bottles—thanks to Crushpad, a Northern California–based winery that makes completely customized wines.

For a set cost of between $5,700 and $10,500 (or about $19 to $35 per bottle), people anywhere can work with Crushpad to create their very own wine label. Clients participate every step of the way, from deciding which grape variety and vineyard they want to use, to working with Crushpad's in-house graphic designers to craft unique labels for their bottles. Clients, who hail from all over the world, typically fly into the California winery several times during the wine's creation to participate in any step of the process they want, including pressing the grapes, tasting the juice and blending the mixtures. In between visits, clients can oversee the production of their wine from anywhere in the world through innovative software the company spent more than $3 million to create.

"There are millions of people who want to quit their jobs and move to Napa Valley—it's the new American dream," Crushpad's founder Michael Brill told me. "This is the next best thing."

That is certainly true for Rick and his wife, Wanda, who have now made three custom wines with Crushpad, and have even launched a small successful business with their private label. As Rick said, "We drink about half of the wine we make ourselves and sell the other half to family and friends. One of our biggest clients is actually my nephew, who is a chef in Kansas. I started out doing it for fun, but now, with three seasons behind us, I've caught the winemaking bug and gotten really passionate and serious about it." Rick's expertise is obvious from the way he talks about winemaking, which is so detailed that he actually lost me several times as he described the process. It was a mouthwatering description though, and I'll definitely be lining up to buy a bottle of their latest vintage.

Rick's expertise demonstrates that in this custom age you simply don't have to be rich and retired to be a true winemaker. Indeed, professional winemaking with Crushpad is such a popular business model that, when all is said and done, Crushpad manufactures roughly 1 percent of all wine labels available in the United States today.

Step 5: Choose Your Company Name, Buy Your Website and Officially Register Your Business

In the internet world, the key to choosing a company or product name is to make sure you can buy the Web domain for it, and that it is a relatively uncommon word or phrase so that you will come up close to the top of the page when someone does a Google search for your company. Also, make sure it's easy and straightforward to pronounce and spell. We originally chose to call our nutrition bar company Fed-Up Bars because we were "fed up" with mass-produced bars. We quickly discovered that it was negative in tone and did not suggest the personalized nature of what we were doing.

At NetworkSolutions.com and GoDaddy.com, you can simply type in your desired domain name (your website's URL) and find out if it's available. If it is, you can click through to buy it for around $10 a year, and spend $9 a month for hosting (see Step 6 for more engaging hosting options). You will probably want to trademark your product name at some point, so simultaneously check the United States Patent and Trademark Office (www.uspto.gov/trademarks/) to use its free Trademark Electronic Search System (TESS) to search if someone else is using that trademark in a similar category.

Once you've done those basic searches and obtained your website, it's time to make your company official, including setting up your business entity (e.g., partnership or corporation). For an easy one-stop shop, go to LegalZoom.com. LegalZoom can also help you with a more complete search and filing for your trademarks.

At the same time, go online to your city, county and state government offices and chamber of commerce for essential information regarding business licenses, possible sales tax collection requirements and "doing business as" (DBA) filings (if necessary). If your business involves food, you will also need to contact the local health department. My cofounder took a half-day class at a local community college on how to start a business in Los Angeles, which provided useful information and emphasized the benefit of seeking qualified legal and accounting advice early in the process of starting a business to avoid costly mistakes. When we first launched YouBar, the luckiest break we had in this arena was that my good friend David Fuad, a Los Angeles-based lawyer, very generously offered his first-rate legal advice free of charge.

Step 6: Create Your Website

In the internet world, your website *is* your storefront. That's great for your rent bills. Unfortunately, that dream website you want will cost the same amount as building a dream store. Configurators, the Web tools that allow customers to design their own products online, still typically cost $10,000, even for the most affordable ones. The designers responsible for Reebok's top-of-the-line, 3-D-view–equipped custom sneaker website told my coauthor that simply adding the interactive designs and images of one new shoe to the website costs between $25,000 and $50,000.

But there is good news. When you're first starting out, you don't need a configurator. You just need a great-looking, functional website. One excellent company that shows just how alluring a CIY company can be without any online design tools is British tea customizer Blends for Friends. Owner Alex Probyn, a master tea blender in his own right, launched the company in 2007 when he saw an opening in the market for people to get teas suited to their precise personalities. On the Blends for Friends website, there is a form that allows the buyer to type in his name, personality traits and hopes for the perfect tea, and then Alex uses his long-honed expertise (he's made more than 10,000 teas) to turn these ideas into a real tea with a unique personalized label.

Blends for Friends' website is classy, functional and successful—the company has seen sales double every year since launching. In 2011 it opened its first brick-and-mortar store in Selfridges, a luxury department store in London, to complement the company's online presence. "There's a pride factor to the tea," Alex said, "At the next dinner party my clients have, they can bring it out and say, 'This is the tea I made.'"

Making your own website with similar functionality to Alex's is easier than ever. As always, it is possible to do it yourself from scratch if you (or a business partner/friend) have a moderate level of Web design experience, particularly with the open-source (free) Web design software Drupal (drupal.com). However, there are several new companies that provide everything necessary to build a beautiful, unique website, with excellent functionality and ongoing support—and you'll need absolutely zero Web expertise. Three that I recommend are BigCommerce, Shopify and Goodsie. Starting at around $20 per month, these companies will hand you the tools to design a unique site that exemplifies your brand and the software you need to make credit card and debit card sales. It also links your site to social networking websites, provides automated marketing and ensures that your virtual store shows up on Google searches, among other things.

While neither BigCommerce nor Shopify includes configurators in their design toolboxes, they do give you the ability to allow your customers to engage with you for customization and personalization through text boxes, much like Alex does with his tea. If you start with BigCommerce or Shopify and later decide you want to add a configurator, it is possible to hire a Web designer to modify your site without having to start over.

This could prove particularly appealing as early as 2013. A team of European Web companies, which includes cyLEDGE,[4] has developed a brand-new type of configurator software that, as soon as it launches, will be *free* to integrate into your website. The platform, which is called Combeenation, promises to revolutionize the online marketplace by making online design tools (aka configurators) available to any-sized company with any-sized budget. In the same vein as other hugely successful ecommerce solutions, like PayPal, Combeenation will charge users a percentage of sales to use the configurator. Up-front costs to sellers will be zero, meaning that if you don't make any sales, you don't owe anything. Beta-testing of Combeenation began in the summer of 2012, and a full rollout is planned for 2013.[5]

In addition to your website, it is also important to have a presence on at least one of the booming online marketplaces. These online marketplaces are the virtual versions of popular shopping malls, each with a different style, target market and product type. eBay was the early pioneer in this and it is, of course, still the largest. But, while eBay is excellent for many things, it is terrible at allowing sellers to build their brands. All of eBay's virtual stalls look identical; the only space for differentiation is in product photos, and there is no space to offer customization.

The next generation of online marketplaces fixes that. Three of the biggest names right now are Etsy (for crafts), Foodzie (for artisan food) and ArtFire (for art). These types of sites will help you build your brand by allowing you some control over the look of your stall. Plus, the vibe of all these sites replicates the feeling of being in a boutique store for customers. And they all work well with custom products. Many sellers on these websites ask shoppers to indicate what type of personalization or customization they would like in the prominent "notes" section of the sales page. Typically, these marketplaces charge sellers a modest monthly fee and/or take a small percentage of sales (like eBay).

Finally, it is important for every company today to have a Facebook page, a LinkedIn profile and a Twitter account (for more information of the full impact that social media has for customizers, see chapter ten).

Step 7: Launch Your Business! (You Don't Even Have to Quit Your Day Job)

Now that you have your website up and working, and your initial production method secured, you're ready to launch! Here's when things get really exciting!

The key to this step is to generate as much buzz as possible about your new business, so pick a launch date that will make sense for your company (late spring for custom ice cream, late autumn for custom snowboard accessories). Also, make sure your date isn't already taken by another big event, like an election or a big sporting event.

Once you have your chosen date, get ready to *tell everyone* with emails, press releases, text messages, Facebook and Twitter posts, targeted online advertising and several well-placed phone calls to the most relevant journalists. If that sounds like a lot, it is, but don't worry. The launch will be broken down into three totally manageable stages.

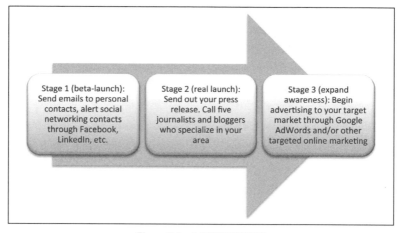

Figure 7.4 LAUNCH STAGES

Stage One: Tell Your Personal Contacts

Web designers call the period right after a website goes live the "beta launch." With big companies, this is often a test phase when only select insiders can use the site. The idea is to get the problems ironed out of your sales platform and your production and shipping methods before journalists, bloggers and reviewers see it. For small startups, this first stage is when you announce your company's opening to your network of friends, family and acquaintances by sending out an email—make sure to include a link to your website. You should also send a Facebook message to all your Facebook friends with a similar announcement and ask them to "Like" your company's Facebook page. It is good practice to include a coupon, perhaps for 25 percent off, in both of these formats, and to thank everyone for being part of your early beta launch and for their support.

Depending on the size of your endeavor, the length of your production and delivery and the complexity of your website, it makes sense to do this anywhere between two weeks and one month before your real launch. Be sure to proactively get feedback from your early buyers (which should be easy, as you know them) so you can fix any problems that aren't obvious.

Stage Two: Tell the Media

Write a press release announcing the launch of your new company using the template in this chapter. I've slanted this press release with examples for a new company launch, but kept it generic enough for you to continue using as your company grows because then you will have new press releases to write. Ideally, you should try to send out a new press release (about anything company-related) at least once a month to keep your company in the public eye.

Start by identifying 10 to 20 journalists or bloggers who write about your particular field or share a similar target demographic (make sure you hit both well-known and not-so-well-known writers because you'll be more likely to have success with the latter). Send one copy of your press release to each of these journalists via email and include another one in traditional mail along with free samples of your product and coupons to use on your site. Follow up with a pleasant phone call two to three days later.

Then it's time to make sure everyone sees it. There are dozens of websites now that allow you to post press releases for public consumption. Four of the most user-friendly are PRWeb.com, Free-Press-Release.com, PRLog.org and PR.com. After registering on these sites, you can upload your latest press release, and they'll take care of making sure it is highly visible for journalists interested in your type of business. Best of all, these sites are all free. If you have a little money to spend, and want your press release to be seen even more widely, I think PRNewswire.com is the best site to use. The annual membership fee is $195, and the site is used as source material by a large number of journalists.

If you don't have any experience writing press releases, don't worry. Here's a sample press release you can use as a starting point:

Your Company's Logo (or Name)

Contact: (full name)

Title: (such as Owner, YouBar)

Phone Number: (ideally a cellphone)

Email Address:

PRESS RELEASE

For Immediate Release

Main Headline—It Is Now Possible to Buy Completely Customized [Your Product]

Subhead (optional)—A New Website, [Your Website Name], Allows Customers to Create Their Very Own [Your Product] and [Any Other Enticing Features]

Dateline—This tells your reader (hopefully a news reporter or blogger!) the city and state you are writing the press release from (this should be the city where your company is headquartered), followed by the date written out in long form, such as: LOS ANGELES, July 18, 2012. This is extremely important as it will attract local media to your story and indicate that your story is relevant and timely.

The Lead—The first paragraph of your story, known as the "lead," should entice your reader with a punchy and interesting intro and provide the answers to the classic FIVE W's (who, what, where, when and why). If you're the first-ever company to offer customization of your product, say that! Also, make sure that you include the name of your company and/or your website address in this paragraph. This is key because press releases are read almost exclusively online these days and the link gives your reader the ability to click to your site easily and without having to scan your whole release.

The Body—After the lead paragraph, press releases typically have between three and five paragraphs (400–600 words) to explain the rest of the story. Good press releases are written just like engaging news stories, so like any newspaper article, these paragraphs should be written in what is known in journalism school as "inverted pyramid" form. This means the most important information comes first and the least important comes last. Make sure that you include the keywords that you want to have associated with your company at least five to 10 times in the text to ensure that your press release will pop up on any searches about those topics. (Our keywords, for example, are nutrition bars, energy bars, protein bars and protein shakes.)

The body of your press release should include some quotes. When you're launching a new company, it makes sense to quote the owner/founder/CEO. Make sure to use the third person (even if you're quoting yourself), as in, "People are fed up with having to settle for off-the-shelf nutrition bars full of preservatives and sugar," said YouBar Owner Anthony Flynn. "With YouBar, customers design their very own bars and, because we make every box fresh to order, we never use chemical preservatives."

If the story is about how your company ties into a larger societal trend, like healthy nutrition bars for fighting the obesity epidemic, it could make sense to quote an expert in the field (a dietician, nutritionist, doctor, etc.) or a recent study or report. When launching or promoting a new product line, it can be useful to quote one or two of your clients about the excellent attributes of your new offering.

The final line of your press release should repeat your contact information and URL, like this: For more information about [The topic], please visit [Your website address goes here], or contact [name of Contact person here] at [email address here] or [phone number here].

About Your Company (also known as "The Boilerplate")—This is a description of your company that goes at the end of every release for your company. Reporters can glance at this to get a quick understanding of what exactly your company does. Once you've written your boilerplate, you don't have to do it again unless your company changes. The same one goes on all of your press releases.

Editor's Note—Including an editor's note is optional, but it can be a useful way of letting journalists know that you're happy to provide material for them.

End Mark—This is just a standard formatting procedure. All press releases end with three pound symbols (###), -30- or –end–. Any of those formats is appropriate.

Stay in the News

After your big launch, it is vital that your company stays newsworthy with regular press releases. You can do this by debuting a new product/material/ingredient, hosting a contest (with free product as a prize), tying your company into a recent trend or celebrity endorsement or anything else that will catch the eye of bloggers and journalists.

Here's an example from YouBar of this kind of press release:

CUSTOM ENERGY BARS

Contact: Anthony Flynn   **PRESS RELEASE**
Owner, YouBar   ****For Immediate Release****
(213) 622-2715
media@YouBars.com

New Bacon Energy Bar at YouBars.com Lets Customers Enjoy Nutrition-Packed, Guilt-Free Bacon Breakfast

**YouBar makes energy bars that taste like bacon.
The surprise? They're delicious.**

LOS ANGELES, February 16, 2012—YouBar, a nutrition bar company famous for making fresh, customized energy bars, has just added the "Bacon Bar" to its list of delicious customizable energy bar flavors available at YouBars.com. The Bacon Bar is made with California dates, organic almond butter and maple syrup—with vegan bacon bits scattered throughout. The resulting protein bar tastes like delicious, crisp, salty breakfast bacon in every bite, yet it provides the nutritional punch of the healthiest breakfast possible—it packs in 12 grams of protein and is rich in natural magnesium, potassium, iron and dietary fiber—all at just 190 calories and zero cholesterol.

The idea for the Bacon Bar came straight from one of YouBar's new clients, who is on a weight-loss diet. His nutritionist sent him to YouBar, recommending that he eat YouBar's "Breakfast Bar" every morning in order to shed his unwanted pounds. While he liked the taste of the Breakfast Bar, he missed his daily breakfast of bacon and called YouBar to see if the company had any suggestions.

YouBar Owner Anthony Flynn loved the challenge of making a bar that would satisfy his new customer's bacon-biting palate and began testing recipes that day. "The vegan bacon bits were the magic ingredient," Flynn said. "They provide the perfect crunch and taste of real bacon without adding bad fats, cholesterol and calories. Best of all, while it might seem really weird to have a bacon-flavored energy bar, it actually tastes incredibly delicious. It has become my own favorite breakfast bar!"

From a nutritionist's point of view, the Bacon Bar is also a runaway hit. The protein bar's almond butter provides calcium, magnesium and vitamin E, and even better, almonds have been proven to reduce the risk of heart attack by as much as 50 percent when eaten at least five times per week (or for breakfast every weekday morning). Meanwhile, the Bacon Bar's dates are high in dietary fiber, iron and potassium.

The Bacon Bar will be featured on www.YouBars.com for a limited time for just $2.50 per bar. As with all YouBars, you can completely customize the packaging on the Bacon Bar, making it an incredible gift for anyone on a reluctant diet—whether they're a meat lover or a vegan who likes a meat taste. Bacon bits are now also available for all YouBar's customers to incorporate into other totally customized nutrition bars, so they can mix them with any of their favorite YouBar ingredients. YouBar's totally customized boxes of nutrition bars start at just $2.99 per bar.

For more information about Bacon Protein Bars, please visit www.YouBars.com or contact YouBar at media@youbars.com or (213) 622-2715.

About YouBars.com—YouBar makes fresh, customized energy bars, protein shakes and trail mixes. At YouBar, we use only the freshest all-natural ingredients. We personally source all our ingredients to ensure that they are preservative-free and provide maximum flavor and nutritional benefit.

Editor's Note—YouBar product samples and photos are available on request.

--end--

Stage Three: Tell Your Target Market

When Jan-Christoph Goetze launched PersonalNOVEL he searched for websites that had readers in his key target market and then paid several of those websites to place small banner ads on their websites linking to his. That was a great plan back in 2003, and it was successful. Thankfully for us, though, online advertising has come a long way since then.

Now, all you have to do to get the kind of advertising that Jan-Christoph had to search and bargain for is to go to Google AdWords (AdwordsGoogle.com). Simply sign up and tick the boxes of exactly the type of customer you would like to target (gender, age, etc.). Google will use the extensive knowledge it has of people who use its search engine, based on the types of searches they conduct, to put banner ads for your company up on the computer screens of members of your precise target market. There are, of course, other companies that do this type of online advertising, including Yahoo!, Microsoft and Facebook. But Google is by far the largest, controlling a full 46 percent of the market.[6] So, as a starting point, go to Google.

You can purchase Google AdWords' online advertisements in two distinct ways. Traditional banner ads cost $3 to $5 per 1,000 times your ad appears. This is called cost per thousand (CPM). The other method of buying these ads is known as pay per click (PPC). With PPC, you are only charged for the advertisement if the person the ad was shown to clicks on the advertisement to link to your page. So, if no one goes directly to your website from the ad link, you don't pay anything.

The pricing for this is slightly more complex. It is worth experimenting with both CPM and PPC to see which is a better fit for your brand. To determine this, check what percentage of people who see your CPM ad click through to your website (this is known as the "click-through rate," or CTR). If you have a high CTR, then CPM (also known as "impression advertising") is best for you. However, if you have a low CTR, then PPC advertising is the best choice.

KEY ONLINE ADVERTISING TERMS	
Common Term	**Definition**
CPM (Cost Per Thousand), also known as "Impression Advertising"	Traditional banner ads. When using these, you will typically pay $3 to $5 for every one thousand times your ad appears.
PPC (Pay Per Click)	These look the same as the above CPM banner ads. The difference is in pricing. With PPC, you only pay when a customer clicks on your ad to go to website.
CTR (Click-Through Rate)	The percentage of time that consumers click on your CPM ads.

The online advertiser that we're most excited about at YouBar right now is Facebook. Facebook ads offer clients the ability to target even more specific *custom* markets than Google because the social media giant's knowledge of your potential customers is based on users' Facebook profiles. With Facebook ads, you can target fans of specific TV shows or even people on their birthdays. In the long run, the intensely customized advertising that social media platforms have could ultimately allow them to offer the holy grail of advertising: You don't get charged unless the person advertised to actually *buys* your product.

■ Useful Information

When you're ready to launch your custom business, it is important to know if other customizers already exist in the field and also get ideas on which existing companies might be able to help with your production and packaging. For this, go to CustomNation.com's Company Customizer to get completely customized, up-to-date information, including:

- ◆ The names of the other custom companies operating in your category of goods.
- ◆ A list of companies that actually produce those types of goods in-house, as these companies could potentially be good to outsource production to.

- ◆ A list of all the social media websites that your target demographic is currently frequenting en masse.

If you are launching a custom food company, please make sure to read the afterword, which includes extensive food industry-specific data and case studies.

For more information about the companies discussed throughout this book, visit CustomNation.com/Companies.

CHAPTER 8

Adding CIY to Your Existing Business

Dozens of the world's largest retail giants, including Ford, Burberry, Hallmark, Levi Strauss, Louis Vuitton, Disney and PepsiCo, still rely on mass production for the majority of their sales. But they're also starting to sell customized goods. As these behemoths of capitalism demonstrate, companies gain significant benefits through launching CIY product lines (even if they only make up a small portion of total sales). Because of my success with YouBar, I have consulted with a number of traditional firms with mass-production models to help them launch their own lines of custom goods. As a result, I know firsthand what obstacles big companies run into when they start doing customization, but I also know the benefits. And they're remarkable.

In fact, because customization is itself such a flexible concept, encompassing everything from completely built-to-order to simple personalized packaging, I believe that every company—no matter what the business model, size or scope—can reap enormous rewards from it. Here are the *nine phenomenal benefits* you are almost guaranteed to achieve simply by adding even a small dash of CIY. The case studies I use to illustrate these benefits show that customization doesn't mean you have to change your fundamental business model or risk alienating your existing clients. If you're the owner of a company, I think this chapter will convince you that it is time to empower your clients with design. If you work for a large firm, try pitching a version of this list to your boss with your own great idea for the custom addition that would suit your company. It will definitely get them thinking, and, who knows, it just might get you promoted.

In fact, because customization is itself such a flexible concept, encompassing everything from completely built-to-order to simple personalized packaging, I believe that every company—no matter what the business model, size or scope—can reap enormous rewards from it.

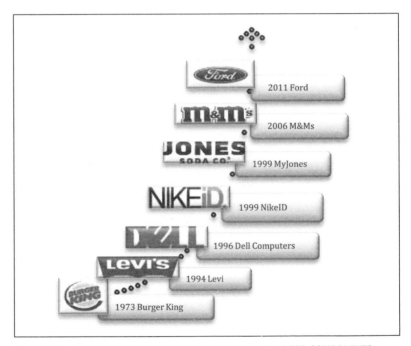

Figure 8.1   LARGE, ESTABLISHED COMPANIES THAT HAVE ADDED COMPONENTS OF CUSTOMIZATION

■ 1. Free Publicity

By adding even a small CIY section to your company's retail offering, you give journalists from all sizes of publications (from *Vogue* to the local blogger) a hot topic to cover in their next article. Take, for example, the global luxury brand Louis Vuitton. In 2010, the company launched the Mon Monogram line in its online store, allowing customers to put their *own* monograms and uniquely colored stripe designs on the brand's classic bags and suitcases.

For Louis Vuitton's brand, the launch of Mon Monogram was successful even before the company sold anything. The new feature generated *thousands* of articles for LV, landing column inches in all the most esteemed style bibles—*Vogue, Marie Claire, Style*—and glowing reviews from the top fashion blogs, including Polyvore, Justluxe and Redcarpet-Fashionawards. "Now you can get your own unique piece of luxury," *Vogue* gushed. The glossy's Web story even included a link to Louis Vuitton's home page, sending readers straight to all of the brand's offerings, not just the personalized section. The free press didn't stop there. Customization is hot with the biggest brand-boosting celebrities too. Gwyneth Paltrow, Lily Allen, Katie Holmes and Sienna Miller have all been photographed carrying their own Mon Monogram bags.

The free press doesn't just work for high-end brands; it works for everyone. In 2011, Frommer's, the travel guide company, launched "Remix Guides." These fun, CIY guides allow customers to go online to Frommer's website, choose where they're going (from dozens of cities), what they love (say, pasta and beaches) and what they don't (say, museums and expensive hotels), and get their very own custom travel guide printed just for them with their own cover (saying, for instance, "Emily and Anthony's Trip to Dubai"). The Remix Guides were a megahit with the travel press, getting great write-ups everywhere from *The New York Times* to the niche culture-lover's website, ArtWorldTravel.com.

■ 2. Higher Prices

The majority of the most successful large-scale customizers strive to make the price point of their products on par with similar mass-produced products. At YouBar, for example, our fully customized bars start at $2.89—the same amount you'd pay for top-of-the-line organic nutrition bars at retailers like Whole Foods. FashionPlaytes, the company that invites preteens to custom design their own clothes, prices their items similarly to Gap.

That said, consumers *are willing* to pay a premium for custom goods, especially from high-end established brands. According to a 2011 study by NPD Group, most customers are happy to spend around 25 percent more to get goods built specifically to their needs, although the premium varies widely depending on the product and the type of customization. Many high-end brands can even command as much as a 50 to 100 percent premium for giving customers the luxury of a custom item. Louis Vuitton's classic Keepall 50 bag costs $1,170 off-the-rack, while the customized Mon Monogram version commands a $1,580 price tag. Likewise, Burberry, which launched a line of totally customizable, made-to-order trench coats in 2011, sells its ready-to-wear trench coats starting at $750. Comparable customized ones start at more than double that number: $1,795.[1]

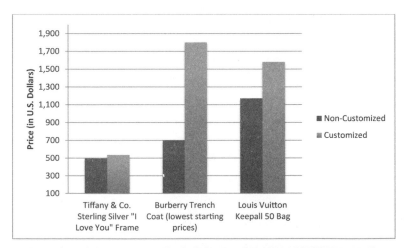

Figure 8.2   SAMPLE PRICES FOR CUSTOMIZED AND NON-CUSTOMIZED ITEMS FROM ESTABLISHED HIGH-END BRANDS

■ 3. Free Market Research

When The Walt Disney Co. made a deal with Zazzle to allow Zazzle's consumers to use Disney's extensive catalog of characters (from Mickey Mouse to Buzz Lightyear) in its custom designs of everything from T-shirts to posters, Disney thought it would be a fun way to include its young fans in the creative process. What Disney might not have realized was that it would also gain invaluable market research from the deal.

That became obvious when Disney's celebrated movie production company Pixar, the maker of *Toy Story*, *Finding Nemo*, and *Up*, came out with its blockbuster children's movie *Cars* in 2006. As always with its big-budget movies, Disney licensed a dizzying array of mass-produced *Cars*-branded merchandise: lunchboxes, toy cars, sheets, beds, tables, backpacks, silverware, toilet seats—the list goes on and on. The vast majority of what it made featured the hero of *Cars*, the racecar Lightning McQueen. And the merchandise sold extremely well.

But on Zazzle, something else was happening. Customers were making designs with Lightning McQueen, but they were also creating merchandise that *just* featured Lightning's loyal tow-truck sidekick, Mater. In fact, fans were creating so many Mater-only designs that Pixar realized there was a mainstream Mater market. It's basically a giant "vote-with-your-wallet focus group," Zazzle's then Brand Director Andy Howell told us. So Pixar launched a line of Mater goods that also racked up enormous sales. The two-pronged approach clearly paid off. Since 2006, the *Cars* franchise has sold more than *$10 billion* worth of retail products worldwide. That puts *Cars* up there with *Star Wars*, *Harry Potter*, and *Spider-Man* for jackpot merchandising.

■ 4. A Bigger Slice of the Gift Market

Americans spend an estimated $40 billion a year on Christmas gifts alone.[2] Add birthdays, anniversaries, Mother's Day, Valentine's Day and the myriad other gift-giving events, and that number balloons. Americans love giving gifts with a personal touch, and adding elements of customization or personalization transforms otherwise mundane items into extremely thoughtful, personal gifts. A box of chocolates becomes a love letter (with chocri), a picture frame becomes an heirloom (with Tiffany & Co.'s engraving), and even a nutrition bar becomes a thoughtful Mother's Day gift (with YouBar).

Hallmark proved that the same customization magic also works with children's books. In 2009 Hallmark landed a *hallmark success* when it launched a "recordable storybook" for the Christmas season. The company put out *The Night Before Christmas* with an integrated recorder linked to page turning that would allow people to *read* the story to children dear to them, even if they lived far away. It was such a huge success that it sold out within weeks. Since then Hallmark has published 21 more recordable storybook titles, some with integrated background music. The books made up the central display areas at Hallmark stores across the world for the 2011 holiday season. Best of all, even though the recordable storybooks are classic CIY (people record *their own* voices into the books), the books themselves aren't sold with any unique personalization, so they haven't changed Hallmark's mass-production business model, showing that big established companies *can* do CIY with no production changes—if they get creative.

Interestingly, imbuing products with custom elements increases their gift appeal whether they're relatively inexpensive products (like Hallmark books) or extremely expensive. For proof, there's no company better than Blue Nile, the online diamond jeweler that specializes in custom engagement rings. In 1999, Blue Nile launched with the then revolutionary idea that people would flock to buy engagement ring diamonds online because it would give them much greater choice and cut out the middlemen jewelry retailers, giving buyers much better deals (Blue Nile sells its diamonds at around 20 percent above cost, compared to the more than 40 percent markup that most shopping mall jewelers charge). At first, the business plan was dismissed by many industry insiders as ridiculous—people might be willing to buy cheap stuff like books and CDs online, they reasoned, but not diamonds.

They couldn't have been more wrong. In 2007, Blue Nile's finance chief, Diane Irvine, told *The New York Times* that the average diamond Blue Nile sells costs $5,500 but that it also sells as many as a dozen diamonds a month that are so expensive—$50,000 or more—that delivery is done via armored trucks with armed guards.[3] By 2012 the company was worth $555 million.

GO NUTS WITH CUSTOMIZATION

The lessons from this chapter aren't just for big business. Even if you run a small, family business, adding an element of customization can increase profits.

Consider the story of the Newark Nut Co. In 1929, Sol Braverman, a 22-year-old Jewish immigrant from Poland, started the brand on a small bank loan, selling nuts and dried fruit on Mulberry Street, a popular open-air market in Newark, N.J. The company grew impressively and became a booming business under the direction of Sol's two sons by the 1970s.

As the century started coming to an end, however, the business started struggling. It desperately needed a revamp to keep up with the modern consumer's desires. Luckily, Sol had a grandson who had inherited his flair for entrepreneurship. In 2003, more than 70 years after the Newark Nut Co. first opened its doors, Jeffrey Braverman, Sol's 22-year-old grandson, left his job as an investment banker in New York City to take over the ailing family business. "I wanted to do something a bit more fulfilling," Jeffrey said.

He renamed it Nuts.com, relaunched it online and started suggesting customized trays of nuts, dried fruit, candies and chocolates as great gifts. By 2006 Jeffrey had transformed his family's struggling nut and dried fruit company into a multimillion-dollar national success story with 75 employees. "There were a lot of times when I was growing up when we weren't sure what was going to happen with the business," said Jeffrey. "Not anymore."

▌5. More Repeat Sales with Lower Return Rates

By giving your customers control over the design of your products, they'll get exactly what they want *and* they'll feel more connected to the end product, which will translate directly into repeat sales. Stuffed animals aren't an industry that is traditionally big on repeat customers. But Build-A-Bear Workshop Inc. changed that when it launched as the world's first *custom* teddy bear retailer. The company, which allows its pint-sized customers to create their very own teddy bears, was built on the idea that children would love their teddy bears more if *they* helped make them.

Founder Maxine Clark's vision paid off. By 2007, 10 years after the company launched, it had sold more than 50 million stuffed animals and had more than 400 stores around the globe.

The true devotion children feel toward the stuffed animals they make at the stores has been the engine behind the company's growth. The origin of stuffed animals hasn't traditionally been an important factor in their sales. But with Build-A-Bear Workshop, that changed. A full 60 percent of the company's guests are repeat customers who plan their store visits in advance. At the time of this writing, this phenomenal customer loyalty had translated into the company being worth $81 million. Consumers themselves are also increasingly aware that this is the kind of individuality they want: More than 35 percent of online consumers in the United States report being interested in customizing product features and buying made-to-order goods.[4]

Not only does customization secure repeat sales, it also dramatically reduces return rates on products. CafePress customizes all sorts of products for the consumers of large brands, like SIGG water bottles and Gaiam yoga mats. CafePress' CEO Bob Marino told me that the large brands CafePress works with report that the percentage of time consumers return their goods after having them customized by CafePress typically plummets (compared to the exact same non-custom good).

6. Stronger Online Presence . . . and a More Personal Connection to Your Customers

Offering customization will give your customers a reason to come to your website instead of just buying your product in stores. The benefits of this are enormous. The more people who come to your website, and the longer they spend on your site, the higher you'll be ranked by all the leading search engines like Google and Yahoo! This will mean that when someone searches for items that you sell, you'll come up toward the top of the search, leading to a virtuous cycle of new customers.

Balance Bar, for example, is a significantly bigger company than YouBar (it sold more than $120 million of bars in 2009). But if you Google the terms "energy bar" or "nutrition bar," you'll find that we always make the first page of search results, while Balance Bar always comes up after us. Similarly, type the words "greeting card" into a Google search, and 123greeting, an online company that specializes in custom e-cards comes up before Hallmark. (It is worth noting that Hallmark is doing an excellent job of increasing its custom online options, and I would guess that Hallmark will succeed at topping the search chart again soon.)

What's more, when people come to your website, you have the opportunity to offer them a coupon if they'll "like" you on Facebook. When someone's already online, this only takes them a second of their time. Getting "liked" on Facebook means that when any of that individual's Facebook friends come to your website, which happens frequently with large companies, your website will automatically come up with their own friends' Facebook profile pictures recommending you.

In addition to this, when a customer "likes" you on Facebook, then anything you post to your Facebook page will come up in their Facebook newsfeed. This is a great way of remaining at the top of your customers' minds, and creating a kind-of personal connection with your customers. Josh Elman, the venture capitalist we talked to in chapter two, said that being present on social networks gives your brand the human touch. "People want to anthropomorphize brands," he told us. "A [good] brand is more of a friend . . . Their goal is to engage [potential] customers in conversation."

PEOPLE OVER PROFIT

CafePress, the custom-everything company worth $288 million, is enormously successful because it's not just focused on sales; it is also a bustling community of designers who collaborate and share their ideas on the website. As a result, CafePress and its sister properties attract more than 11 million unique visitors every month. In the modern business world, popularity itself is often starting to matter as much as sales, profits or anything else. Case in point: When Google bought YouTube in 2006 for $1.65 billion, YouTube had (according to analyst estimates) just $15 million a year in revenue and had never turned a profit.

7. The Ability to Sell Directly to Consumers without Making Your Retailers Mad

Have you ever wondered why many of the biggest mass producers, like Kraft and Bosch, have websites that won't let you buy anything? If you work for a large company, you'll already know the answer: They don't want to make the giant retailers who sell their products, like Walmart and Target, angry by competing with them directly for sales. While producers would, of course, make more money on their direct sales to customers (because they wouldn't have to pay a percentage to the retailer), the advantage of these higher margins is wiped out by the risk of losing their shelf space in places like Walmart.

In the business world, the problems that arise when producers compete with their own retailers to sell the same products are called "channel conflicts." Traditionally, the way around these conflicts was simply for producers not to sell their products at all. But another way for producers to avoid channel conflicts is to sell a *different* product from the one they supply to their retailers. In the online world, customization is (of course!) the obvious answer.

The most classic example of this comes from Nike. The company itself has gone on record to say that one of the main reasons it first launched its custom sneaker website, NikeID.com, was so that it could start selling its shoes directly to consumers—and increase its online presence—without angering its retailers. This proved to be a hugely successful strategy. NikeID.com receives nearly 1 million page views every single day, and it sold more than $100 million of custom shoes in 2010 alone. Needless to say, the company didn't have to give any of this money to middlemen retailers.

■8. Greater Customer Loyalty

Procter & Gamble might not be the first company that comes to mind when you think of customization. Pampers diapers and Tide detergent are modern icons of mass production. But like so many of the smartest big brands, P&G is actually doing some impressive work in the custom realm and getting incredible results. There are a number of P&G programs I could use to illustrate this point, including a personalized cosmetics line it offers through OlayForYou.ca, but my favorite is the company's foray into health care.

In 2009 P&G took complete ownership of MDVIP, a health care provider that focuses on "personalized health care"—meaning doctors on the plan customize health plans (diet, exercise, etc.)—for their patients to prevent instead of treat illness. Doctors at MDVIP consider their patients' entire lives to develop an idea of what they can do to keep them healthy. This stands apart from the standard model of a doctor seeing a patient after he already has a problem, and then treating it with a standard pill designed for a generic problem that seems the probable cause. Although the company is still relatively young, it has already attracted 175,000 patients, and its loyalty rates are among the highest in health care. It boasts a 92 percent renewal rate and a 96 percent satisfaction rate.

SAYING YES TO CREATE LOYAL CUSTOMERS

Increasing customer loyalty through customization is something that every company can do—whether old or new. Consider, for example, Poquito Mas, one of LA's hippest chain restaurants. CEO Kevin McCarney founded the quick-service Mexican restaurant back in 1984 on just $11,000. He is now the head of a dozen-strong chain, whose fresh tortillas are so delectable that there are often lines running out of the door. Kevin said that since launching, customization has "absolutely" become more and more important to his customers. "We train our staff to say yes," Kevin said. Yes to weird combos, odd ingredients and different sizes. He said you can't run a successful food business today without making sure that customers get exactly what they want. He said, "If you don't say yes to customers, they will go to someone who will."

■ 9. More Sales

As we discussed in depth in chapter three, millennials (13- to 31-year-olds) have grown up with customization like never before and expect it in every aspect of their lives. As a result, companies that don't offer custom products will inevitably lose consumers accustomed to getting customization.

Jason Lucash knows this better than most. In 2009, Jason, a 28-year-old Californian entrepreneur, invented high-quality speakers that could fold flat for traveling. Within three months of putting these OrigAudio collapsing speakers on the market, they were named one of "The 50 Best Inventions of 2009" by *Time*. Jason's company took off, and he immediately followed up with another megahit called the Rock-It, an amazing piece of technology the size of a film canister that turns any object (a box, a book, a car, anything!) into a speaker just by sticking his device on it.

OrigAudio's revenues shot through the roof—to "multimillions"—but Jason had one problem. "Customers, especially younger customers, wanted custom speakers and we didn't sell them," he said. "We turned away so much business in the first year." But Jason fixed the problem in year two, launching Cubicool, high-quality speakers the shape of giant dice that can be customized with customers' own photos on each of their four sides. Cubicool speakers were an immediate hit, selling 55,000 in the first 12 months on the market. He followed these up with the world's first-ever custom-designed, over-the-head earphones in January 2012.

"When I want something, I want it customized," he said. "I'm even making custom Keds for my groomsmen to wear in my wedding party."

CUSTOMIZATION LITE

Design competitions are an easy way for companies to start getting consumers involved in creating without true customization.

Just because your company isn't ready to start creating truly custom products for consumers doesn't mean you can't start dipping your company fountain pen into consumer creativity. Design competitions are a great way to do this. In this chapter is my favorite case study in that genre. It demonstrates just how profitable adding even a relatively small component of consumer creativity can be for a large company with a fairly standard mass-production business model.

In 2008 Walkers, a giant British potato chip maker owned by PepsiCo's Frito-Lay, ran an amusingly named competition: "Do Us a Flavour!" The contest called for chip lovers to come up with their own ideas for a new flavor (they didn't have to come up with the recipe). In the three months the contest ran, Walkers received an astonishing 1.1 million entries![5]

The huge number of consumers rushing to Walkers online to enter the contest made the company's website the fastest-growing website in Britain in July 2008.[6] The six off-the-wall flavors Walkers chose as finalists earned loads of press in major newspapers and on television, as journalists fell over themselves

CONTINUES

CONTINUED

for the chance to write about chips flavored like "Cajun Squirrel," "Fish & Chips," and "Chilli and Chocolate." More than 800,000 consumers went online to vote for their favorite flavor.

The competition's winner, a 27-year-old English midwife, ultimately won with the flavor "Builder's Breakfast" (a mélange of bacon, buttered toast, eggs and tomato sauce), and took home 50,000 UK pounds (roughly $78,000) and 1 percent of all future sales of the flavor. In the end, though, Walkers was the biggest winner. The contest drummed up press coverage worth an estimated 4.7 million UK pounds ($7.4 million). The brand's equity rose 6 percent. And, year-over-year sales shot up by 14 percent.[7] Definitely customization lite at its best.

Walkers is one of dozens of large brand names asking customers to become involved through such "idea" contests. Here are some others. Ben & Jerry's Ice Cream clocked more than 100,000 flavor entries from 15 different countries with its similarly named "Do the World a Flavor" contest. Dunkin' Donuts' first design contest in 2009 generated nearly 130,000 doughnut submissions. Mountain Dew's first DEWmocracy contest in 2008 clocked 350,000 votes,[8] and better still, resulted in a best-selling drink ("Mountain Dew Voltage").

Even when a prize isn't offered, giving consumers the ability to express themselves on your website can be golden. Starbucks, for example, offers a create-your-own drink experience at Frappuccino.com. Visitors can customize a Frappuccino drink and post it to a gallery or to their Facebook profile. More than 72,000 customer creations have been posted to the Frappuccino.com gallery so far. And the only reason consumers are doing it is to have *fun*.

If you are adding a customizing element to a food company, please make sure to read the afterword, which includes extensive food industry-specific data and case studies.

For more information about the companies discussed throughout this book, visit CustomNation.com/Companies.

CHAPTER 9

The Seven Crucial Lessons of Customizing

This book is filled with company case studies, lists and charts. But when you're planning to launch an actual business, it can sometimes be nice to cut through all the examples and background data and simply see the big picture. So in this chapter I aim to do exactly that. I take the detailed information from all the other chapters in this book and boil it down to seven crucial lessons for customizing.

Lesson One: *Do* Compete with Mass Producers in Speed, Quality and Price

When I asked Bob Marino, the CEO of CafePress, what his top rules for customizers were, he knew the answer immediately. "I can give you three things," he said. "Quality, price, speed . . . better, cheaper, faster." This concise list might seem counterintuitive. After all, during the 20th century most attempts at customization failed to compete with mass production in at least one or two of these categories (the rich could get great custom goods, but it was expensive and time-consuming, while the middle class could get cheap, low-quality or DIY customization). But for the 21st century, the rules of the game have changed. Consumers love custom goods, but they *are not* willing to give up the other qualities they've become accustomed to with mass-produced goods in order to get customization.

1. Better

Early examples of affordable mass customization, like the corner print shop that made custom T-shirts for bachelor parties, custom mugs for joke gifts or custom calendars for Christmas presents, never succeeded because their products weren't high quality. T-shirts fell apart, the ink on mugs washed off in the sink and the calendar collages they produced looked like they were made by kindergartners.

In the 21st century, successful customizers make products that at least match the quality of the mass-produced goods sold at retail stores like Gap, Pottery Barn and Target. Indeed, a 2011 survey by Treehouse Logic, which specializes in creating websites for custom products, found that consumers of custom goods rank the quality of the product they buy as the single-most important thing to them—above fit, selection or brand—with nearly 95 percent of consumers saying quality was either "very" or "extremely" important to them.

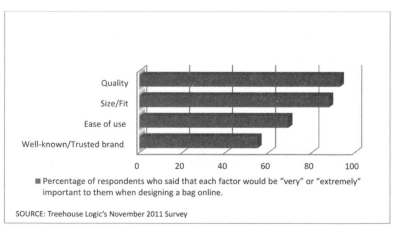

■ Percentage of respondents who said that each factor would be "very" or "extremely" important to them when designing a bag online.

SOURCE: Treehouse Logic's November 2011 Survey

Figure 9.1   TREEHOUSE LOGIC'S SURVEY RESULTS

Bob Marino told me that quality is actually even more important than "extremely" when it comes to custom goods. "The quality has to be *better* than a mass-produced item," said Bob. "If someone took the time to tell you that this is how they want it, they have imprinted passion. So execution matters more than it would have at any other time."

2. Cheaper

Because customization was the preserve of the ultra-rich during the 20th century (with their custom suits, custom art and custom homes), many people still erroneously believe that customizers can charge giant premiums. But in the 21st century, customization will increasingly be an expectation, not exotically elite. While customers will often pay a premium for a custom product, especially from high-end established brands (I have a chart on this in chapter eight), the goal for a good customizer is to try to get the price of its product to match the price of similar mass-produced goods.

A quick glance at the most cutting-edge and successful CIY companies reveals this price structure immediately. ShirtsMyWay and Blank Label sell custom dress shirts for the same price you'd pay for mass-produced brands in typical department stores; CafePress and Zazzle sell custom T-shirts, mugs, wall art and a million other goods for prices competitive with those you'd find at Target; and Blue Nile and Gemvara sell custom jewelry for the same price (or sometimes less) than you'd pay at a shopping mall jeweler. Surveys of consumers support the notion that customizers should aim to keep prices low.

3. Faster

We live in a world of instant gratification, with consumers getting everything from on-demand Netflix movies to Twitter newsflashes *without any waiting*. Even online shopping for goods now delivers near-instant results, with companies like Amazon and Zappos typically delivering goods within a few days, and always offering overnight delivery options. Consumers do want custom goods, but they don't want anything they'll have to wait for.

As a result, successful customizers invest in delivery methods that offer lightning-fast results. The vast majority of the time, as we outlined in depth in chapter five, this means keeping production in the United States, where it's easy and cost-effective to ship quickly.

One great example: Blue Nile, the custom diamond jeweler worth half a billion dollars, offers free overnight delivery on the vast majority of its sales. And it uses this fast service as a marketing tool. The afternoon before New Year's Eve 2012, Blue Nile's website was enticing customers to, "Surprise her with a Signature Diamond on New Year's Eve . . . There's Still Time for a New Year's Engagement." If you ordered a Blue Nile ring before 4 p.m. the day before New Year's Eve, the company guaranteed it would get it to you via free delivery with time to spare before the evening's festivities.

Another great example: When CafePress first launched, it took the company at least 44 hours to ship a custom good. Today it has slashed that to a standard of less than 24 hours for most products. If you buy a custom product from CafePress before 4 p.m. on any given day, you can have it in your hand the very next day. The company has worked hard to increase its speed, even choosing Louisville, Ky., for its main production facility so that it is strategically next door to UPS's headquarters. As Bob put it, "The leaders of the custom revolution are the authentic rule breakers. We're the people who have gone out and said that we can make a custom product faster, cheaper and better than a mass-produced one."

LESSON ONE STRATEGIES

Make something high quality. At the point that you have a prototype of your product, try bringing it into a typical store selling similar goods and literally put it up on the shelf. Look at it next to the other items. Pick it up again after handling the other items. Maybe even (discreetly) ask other customers if anything on the shelf looks out of place. If it feels and looks like it belongs, you have a winner.

CONTINUES

CONTINUED

Deliver as fast as you can. Never assume that your customers will be willing to wait for a custom product. Ideally, in this world of instant gratification, you should strive to deliver your product in the same time as it takes online dealers (like Amazon) of similar mass-produced goods.

Price to compete. Establish who your mass-production competitors are (such as designer handbag brands, department store T-shirts, national brand cereals, etc.) and make your price point goal whatever they charge. You may not be able to start this low, but you should strive to get there.

Produce in the USA (or wherever your customers are). You don't need to make your raw materials, like blank T-shirts or cane sugar, at home, but it is vital to keep the customizing stage of production as close to your consumers as possible so that lightning-fast shipments don't cost more than your actual products. Other benefits of producing at home include such monetary and press-worthy advantages as: 1) Creating jobs in your home economy. 2) Paying no import taxes (even if you import raw materials, import duties on unfinished goods are half those of finished goods). 3) More easily ensure that your staff is well-paid and working in safe conditions. As Mark Dwight, the founder and CEO of Rickshaw Bagworks, the custom messenger bag company with production in San Francisco, put it: Local production "rehumanizes the manufacturing process."

Lesson Two: Provide Exceptional Customer Service

If there was one piece of advice that every single successful customizer we interviewed for this book had for custom entrepreneurs, it was, "Make sure you have obsessively perfect customer service!" Customizers typically don't have physical storefronts because they sell online, so the only way consumers get to interact with people at custom companies—to get recommendations, reassurance and help—is through telephone calls, emails, instant messaging and social media conversations. As a result, it is absolutely vital to provide exceptional and proactive customer service. Zazzle cofounder Jeff Beaver's advice is to treat every single customer "like royalty." At Zazzle, he said, the goal is to "make everyone feel like a rock star."

PersonalNOVEL's CEO Jan-Christoph Goetze told us, "Since we don't have any stores, customer service is the only human face the company has. Great customer service is our *best method of marketing*."

To illustrate just how much Jan-Christoph throws himself into delivering everything for his customers, he told us a story of one evening in the first year of his company:

> I had picked up the books for that night's delivery by bike from the local print shop, and about a block before I made it to the mailbox, I got into a crash because the brake on my bike broke. My knee was bleeding, onlookers were worried, but I still hobbled all the way down to the mailbox to get the books out on time. Since the beginning, the spirit of my company is to do *everything* for the customer.

LESSON TWO STRATEGIES

Make it easy for customers to talk to a *person* to get help. Always have your customer service telephone number highly visible on your website and make sure this line is answered quickly by well-trained staff. Also, your website should give customers the ability to instant message your customer service desk if they don't want to pick up the phone. At YouBar, we've been extremely lucky to have my close friend Joel Lipman heading up our customer service department.

Go above and beyond to keep customers happy. If the rule in standard businesses is "the customer is always right," then the rule for customizing businesses is "the customer is always left." I know it's a silly turn of phrase, but I actually do

CONTINUES

CONTINUED

mean something serious by it: When you make a custom product, you are making it specifically for an individual buyer. You, as a business, aren't left with inventory that you can repackage and resell to other people if a customer isn't happy and returns a product (the way mass producers are), you are *left* with a single consumer-specific item. That is to say, you are left not with resalable inventory but rather with a still-potential customer. If you work hard to re-create the product the customer wasn't happy with so that it becomes exactly what he or she hoped it could be, then you'll be *left with a customer for life.*

Lesson Three: Guarantee Your Customer Will Love What They Get, and Then Guarantee It Again

One sticky problem with customization is that consumers often worry that they won't be very good designers. Even if they love the idea of creating and enjoy the process, they will sometimes stop just before clicking BUY because they're worried that the thing they made won't "turn out right," and that they'll have no one to blame but themselves.

Because of this, it's extremely important for customizers to provide Absolute, 100 Percent, No-Questions-Asked Guarantees that their consumers will like what they get, or else they'll get their money back (and/or get a brand-new "retooled" product that addresses their unmet expectations). In effect, customizers must go out of their way to let customers know that they *only* make great products, and if the customer doesn't absolutely *love* what he receives, then it's not the customer's fault, it's the company's fault. This guarantee should be on the homepage of the website, on the shopping cart page and on an insert inside the package when it is delivered that reiterates it.

If a customer is worried about making a "bad choice" during the buying process, she should be able to contact a customer service person easily and quickly (either online through instant message chat or by telephone) to achieve personal guidance. It is also helpful to install some degree of automated decision-guidance. With chocolate customizer chocri, for example, the software automatically makes ingredient suggestions that pair well with the first ingredients chosen. At YouBar, we have a "Taste Tester" on our website that allows customers to check whether the combination of ingredients they've chosen will likely turn out to be a delicious bar.

Finally, it is absolutely necessary to follow up with each customer after she receives her product. These follow-up emails and phone calls should look for honest feedback and provide free new products (or money back) to anyone not entirely happy with the first thing they received. By doing this, you can turn a person who never would have ordered again into a customer for life.

Make sure your customers *blame you* if they don't like what they get. If you've ever bought a T-shirt at an event—say a band's tour shirt or a baseball team's jersey—and found that it didn't fit quite right or didn't look quite right, you knew precisely where to lay the blame: the manufacturer. I think we've all said things like, "This isn't really a 'large,'" or, "This color is weird." But here's what's interesting. If you've ever bought a T-shirt at a department store, where there were a thousand different T-shirts to choose from (instead of the single design that most event concession stands offer) and found that it didn't fit right or look right, you probably didn't blame the manufacturer or the store; you probably blamed yourself. Instead of saying *they* did something wrong, we typically say things like, "I shouldn't have bought this shirt," or, "I should have tried it on again," or, "I should have known this color would look bad on me."

There's an interesting psychological process underpinning the difference in where we place blame. The more that we feel we've played a part in choosing something, the more we feel that it's our fault if it doesn't turn out right. When we only have one or two choices, we see a bad result as some version of, "The manufacturer made a poor product." When we have dozens of choices, we see a bad result as some version of, "I made a bad decision."

LESSON THREE STRATEGIES

Promise no-hassle returns. Put a big, bold promise on your website that lets customers know that if they don't like what they get—for any reason—they can return it for a full refund. Custom diamond jeweler Blue Nile does this perfectly. On the rotating home page banner of the company's website, one of the central panels reads, "She'll Love it—*Guaranteed.* 30-day returns. No questions asked."

Follow up with your customers and make sure their experiences with your company are perfect. Within one week of delivering their products, make sure to email and/or call customers in order to ensure that they loved what they got. If they didn't love it, send them a new one that fixes the problems and meets or exceeds their expectations.

Lesson Four: Whatever You Do, Don't Give Your Customers Too Many Choices

You can find the full story behind this vital rule in chapter four, but here's the key message: If you give your customers too many choices, the chances that you'll make a sale will drop dramatically. Customers find too much choice overwhelming and often become frozen with indecision. So give your customers a carefully selected and limited number of choices, cut out bad options and always make sure that the choices you give are the fun ones. As Dell found out, for example, people love getting to choose certain things on their computers, like monitor size and software, but they don't want to choose from a whole array of different Bluetooth options. Likewise, customers on the Ford Mustang Customizer website can choose from dozens of hood designs, but they aren't picking the materials used in the engine.

LESSON FOUR STRATEGIES

Decide what your customers enjoy customizing and give choices related to that. By definition, customization of any given object has an almost infinite number of potential choices. Even something as simple as a chair can come in an infinite array of materials, sizes, textures, shapes, colors—the list goes on and on. Focus on the specific components your customers can customize to express their individuality or address health needs and never make the customization options open-ended.

Give customers the option of using a finished design as a starting point to make their own designs. Starting with a completely blank slate can be overwhelming. Try giving customers the option of working off of a finished design that they can tinker with.

Use sequential inclusion rules. If you have a website equipped with configurator technology, it is ideal to put "sequential inclusion rules" in it. This means that every time a customer makes a choice, the following options are limited to work well with the initial one.

Lesson Five: Discover What Emotion Is Driving Your Customers and Cater to That. And Never Sell Your Technology Directly.

Eastman Kodak Co. achieved a near-monopoly on the sales of photographic film products during the 20th century, controlling as much as 90 percent of the U.S. market in the 1970s. However, while Kodak delivered great photographs because of its excellent technology (even with the company filing for bankruptcy protection in 2012, its patents alone are still thought to be worth around $3 billion),[1] the company never marketed itself as a tech genius. Rather, its advertisements all revolved around the underlying emotional reason that consumers loved taking pictures: the lasting memories. And so, Kodak's catchphrase wasn't, "Buy our great silver alloy." It was, "Make it a Kodak moment."

In many ways Kodak was one of the first great customizing companies, as photographs were one of the earliest forms of mass customization. And just like Kodak, today's great customizers are all astutely selling not the technology that enables their customization but rather the emotions their products evoke.

Vistaprint's Robert Keane, who noted Kodak's early customization when we spoke, told me that, like Kodak in its prime, good customizers must "find a way to make their products *resonate* with the end customer." By way of an example, Robert said that for Christmas last year, his wife bought him a custom mouse pad (from Vistaprint of course!), with a photo taken by his daughter of him and his wife walking through a field. "The value of this mouse pad to me is much higher than the value a mouse pad should have," he said. While Vistaprint's proprietary technology is what enabled the mouse pad to look good and function well, the thing that gives it such an elevated value to him is its emotional content. His advice to customizing entrepreneurs is, "Don't be too seduced by the technology of customization."

Matt Lauzon, Gemvara's CEO, is extremely thoughtful about what motivates people to come to his site. "When people buy jewelry, it's an emotional purchase. People want to tell a story with it," he said, "The advice I would give to a new entrepreneur who wants to sell custom goods is to focus on who your customer is and why they want to shop with you."

If you listen for it, you'll hear this same message from successful customizers again and again. In an interview with Small Business Advice TV, Michael Dell, the founder and CEO of computer customizers Dell Inc., told entrepreneurs, "You've got to have a clear articulation of what it is that you offer that's valuable and why it's valuable."[2] Likewise, Brennan Mulligan, a seasoned customizer who founded two technology customization companies, Confego and Skyou, and also manages the supply chain for Reebok's custom shoes, said knowing the customer is the most important advice he would give to anyone who wanted to get into customizing. In an interview, Brennan told me that his top tip is, "Don't focus on products; focus on people."

> "You've got to have a clear articulation of what it is that you offer that's valuable and why it's valuable."
>
> —Michael Dell

LESSON FIVE STRATEGIES

Figure out what really makes customers love your product. While it likely isn't the silver alloy in the photo paper, it probably *is* the "I Love You" engraved on the chocolate bar.

Start with a passionate target market. If you focus on a small, enthusiastic target market, it can often be easier to highlight the value you add by customizing than if you have a larger, more amorphous target audience in mind. Tiny Prints, the custom invitation printer, succeeded because it started with the target focus of birth announcements and expanded from there. Vistaprint started by just making business cards and then added products, like custom mouse pads, business stationery and pens, that would also serve the same small business customers it had cultivated.

WHY CUSTOMIZING MOTIVATES CONSUMERS

By Jeff Beaver

Customization is the single biggest trend in consumerism today because it's what consumers have always wanted and now, thanks to advances in technology (most notably the internet and online design tools), we can finally deliver it for the same price and quality at nearly the same speed as mass production. As a result, consumers are taking hold of their own destinies for the first time in living memory. They're savvy to mass-marketing gimmicks, and they aren't listening to them anymore. So they're not being passively fed stuff as was the norm for the last 100 years. Now they're actively creating and publishing.

CONTINUES

CONTINUED

The core value proposition of this is all personalization. Why is Pandora better than the Top 40 radio station? Because it's made for my tastes. That logic holds true for everything— from cellphones to skateboards.

The reason customization isn't the norm yet is simply because a large percentage of consumers still don't realize they can get custom goods for the same price and same quality as mass-produced goods. One of our main aims at Zazzle is to engender an ecosystem where high-quality customization is the norm for every product. We want to be the Amazon of customization. Once consumers realize they can get a bar that's made specific to their needs or a travel book featuring their own locations or a gift featuring their own photos, there will be no going back. The only question is how fast we can proliferate this message.

Jeff Beaver is the cofounder of Zazzle, the custom-everything company with an estimated value of $275 million.[3]

Lesson Six: Make It Easy for Your Customers to Talk about How Great Your Company Is

One of the central benefits of customizing is that your customers will *want* to talk about your company and share photographs of the products you make because they helped to make them and feel creative ownership over them. Whatever you do, don't squander this incredible source of free marketing and advertising. Instead, make it easy for your customers to brag.

In the modern world, thanks to the explosion in social media websites, customers' social influence has a reach that absolutely dwarfs that of earlier generations. In the past, a person might have 10 or 20 friends that he or she saw on a regular basis. But today, on websites like Facebook and Twitter, individual consumers have literally hundreds of friends and

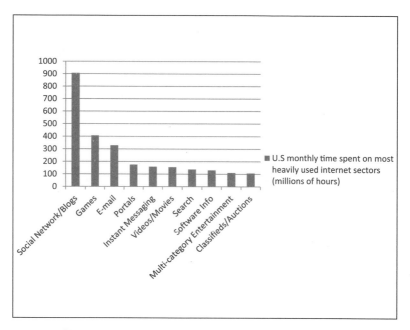

Figure 9.2 U.S. MONTHLY TIME SPENT ON MOST HEAVILY USED
INTERNET SECTORS (MILLIONS OF HOURS)
Source: Nielson NetView, June 2010

followers who they influence on a daily basis. What's more, they spend more time on social networking sites and blogs than on any other online activity. (You can find the full story in the next chapter.)

LESSON SIX STRATEGIES

Put SHARE buttons on your website that allow customers to share the item they've made via social media with the click of a mouse. The SHARE button should ideally allow your customers to share a photograph of what they've created via email, Facebook, Twitter and the other social networking sites your target demographic uses.

CONTINUES

CONTINUED

Cultivate an active presence on the key social networking websites your target market frequents. Have a company Facebook page, deliver company news via Twitter, and offer customers coupons if they "like" you on Facebook or other social media websites. Conduct regular research on which social media sites are popular with your target market, as the space can change fast. It is also ideal to post videos of you and your company in action on YouTube. At YouBar we've been extremely lucky in this category because Adam Mansfield, one of my good friends, is a television producer. With his experience working on shows like *The Bachelor* and *The Bachelorette*, he knows exactly how much modern consumers enjoy getting to know people on reality TV shows. Adam has used his expertise to make us some excellent videos and said that any smart businessperson today would benefit simply by turning a digital camera recorder on themselves and posting the video online. "Consumers expect to know who they are dealing with these days," Adam said, "and not just in professionally edited clips that can seem artificial."

Get help setting up your social networking presence. If you're over the age of 40 or so, try to find someone under that magic number to help you set up your social media websites. Millennials typically use social networking sites on a daily basis and have an intuitive sense of how they function in a way that older consumers (even those who use social networking) typically don't. Getting advice from someone else can also help you come up with great new ideas to use for your social networking presence. The idea for YouBar's Facebook photo contest actually came from one of my brother's friends, Justin Fabillar, a then 23-year-old musician who spent a month looking over what we were doing in the social media world and making suggestions.

▎Lesson Seven: Listen to Your Customers (It's the Key to Growth)

It may seem obvious, but successful customizers spend a lot of time and energy really *listening* to their customers. On the most basic level, they are always engaging in one-on-one dialogue with their clients, whether through CIY software, telephone or email conversations, or social media chat, in order to create exactly the product their customers want. However, this ongoing dialogue also tells customizers exactly how to expand and grow their companies because, as customers engage with creators, they tell those creators what *else* they'd like.

As a result, most of the best customizers today are growing rapidly, inspired by their own consumers. In December 2011, Vistaprint bought Webs Inc., a Maryland-based provider of do-it-yourself websites, Facebook pages and mobile sites, for $117.5 million in cash and shares. The reason for the acquisition wasn't just to gain Webs Inc.'s existing customer base (at the time of purchase, Webs had served more than 40 million customers worldwide and had more than 100,000 paying subscribers) but also to increase its presence as a one-stop shop for small businesses. Webs Inc. allows Vistaprint to offer its small business customers help and guidance in setting up their online shops and company Facebook pages. "We believe in small businesses," Vistaprint CEO Robert Keane told me. "Everything around marketing your small business [is] very related to our core value proposition. Facebook is a big part of making your small business work."

Intriguingly, customer demand has also driven Vistaprint to start expanding into nonbusiness products, like photo gifts and photo books, in order to meet the personal needs of predominantly business clients. "Our traditional focus on business will stay core," said Robert, "but we'll increase our home and family [products]." To that end, just a month before it bought Webs Inc., Vistaprint paid $82 million to acquire Dutch photo book company Albumprinter. Explaining the purchase, Robert pointed to office supply company Staples as a model. Staples, he pointed out, deals primarily in servicing business needs, but is also a go-to destination for back-to-school shopping.

Dozens of other customizers are making giant acquisitions to fund similar consumer-inspired growth. Shutterfly, for example, bought Tiny Prints, an online publishing company that sells cards, invitations, personalized stationery and photo books, which allowed Shutterfly to expand from its core photo gift market into stationery and invitations. Likewise, Zazzle has made several important acquisitions and deals in the last several years— its purchase of custom technology platform Confego, for example—that have allowed the company to start working with custom goods (like Reebok shoes and Laudi Vidni bags) that aren't simply customized through printing personal designs on blank items, but are made to order from more basic parts. CafePress, meanwhile, has purchased several custom art-printing companies, including Canvas on Demand and Imagekind.

The expansion that companies like Shutterfly and CafePress are investing in is excellent for two reasons. First, it makes their customers happy, which is good in and of itself, of course. Second, it's a lucrative strategy for long-term sales. When customers receive high-quality, custom product quickly at a good price from a given brand, it is only natural for them to gravitate to that company to meet their other custom demands, if possible. And this is a golden ticket to long-term company growth— transforming customers from single-product buyers to lifelong clients for a variety of products.

LESSON SEVEN STRATEGIES

Take notes. Keep track of what your customers are asking for, either by phone or email. If lots of customers are looking for the same thing that you don't have, consider expanding. At YouBar, we have a space for customers to write in ingredient requests, and we do our best to source each write-in request. To encourage suggestions, it can make sense to send customers surveys. In 2009, Christian Newth, a good friend of mine who was in business school at USC at the time, created a survey for our customers that gave us an enormous amount of valuable information.

CONTINUES

CONTINUED

Use partners. If you can't offer something that naturally complements your own product or service, make a deal with another company to send customers to each other. For example, if you make custom hiking shoes, it could make sense to find a partner that offers custom hiking accessories (like water bottles and backpacks). Both of you could put links on your own websites to each other, thereby increasing the total number of customers for both of you.

Keep growing. As customization increasingly takes over as the norm for consumer goods and services in the 21st century, there will inevitably be key customizing companies that dominate as the giants in each industry. Frontrunners right now are Vistaprint for businesses, CafePress and Zazzle for consumer retail goods and Shutterfly for gifts. But there is still an enormous amount of room to fill giant gaps. As a result, when you start a customizing business, dream big—and keep growing.

For more information about the companies discussed throughout this book, visit CustomNation.com/Companies.

CHAPTER 10

Customize Your Marketing

I t's no secret. Any good advertising executive today will tell you that a strong social media presence on websites like Facebook, Twitter and LinkedIn is the holy grail of modern sales. Social media sites and blogs now command nearly a quarter of the time Americans spend online—more than email, shopping or any other activity. Nearly 80 percent of internet users in the United States now engage in social media, with roughly 32 million Americans visiting Facebook every single day.[1] And consumers who make connections with brands on social media websites spend 20 percent to 40 percent more money buying their products and services than those who don't.[2] In other words, if you aren't talking to your customers on social media, and your customers aren't recommending you to their friends on social media, you are missing the boat.

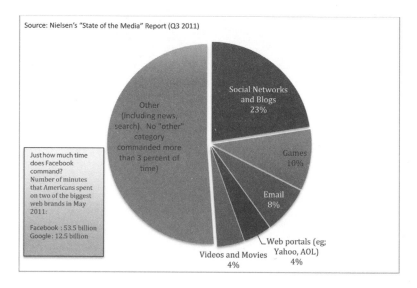

Figure 10.1   PERCENTAGE OF TIME AMERICANS SPEND ON THE MOST
POPULAR ONLINE ACTIVITIES

So, the million-dollar question is: How do you develop a strong presence on social media websites without spending too much money? And the answer is simple (and I'll bet you can guess what I'm going to say): Customize! Last century, expensive TV, magazine and billboard advertisements and costly PR connections to the top journalists were the key tools to getting sales. Not anymore. With social media dominating our time, the most valuable advertisement you can get is free: buzz from your buyers.

And the way to get that is to *give your customers creative ownership* of the product that you make. When your customers are your designers, they'll initiate conversations about what they've created using your service with their friends online. And in the process of doing that—like posting a glossy mock-up of the Mustang they just created at Ford.com, or the sneakers they designed at Vans.com up on their Facebook profile—they'll be talking about you and sending all of their friends, and all of their friends' friends, to your website.

This method is much more valuable than traditional marketing. Ninety percent of people trust recommendations from people they know, and 67 percent of people will spend more money than average on a product when it comes recommended by a friend.[3] Research firm iProspect estimates that Facebook guided the buying decisions of more than 86 million people during the holiday season in 2011, with a clear majority of shoppers—57 percent—using Facebook and Twitter to stay informed on holiday sales and promotions. According to *Entrepreneur* magazine, for some brands, every person who shares content will bring an additional five new unique visitors back to a site. And those visitors will spend 1.3 times longer on the site, read 1.9 times more content and even report that they like the brand more than people who arrive at websites through other paths.[4] In short: Getting your customers to talk about your company on social media sites is the definition of perfect viral marketing. And, best of all, it can cost close to nothing.

CASE STUDY: THREADLESS

Without a doubt, one of the most innovative examples of social media marketing the world has seen comes from a Chicago T-shirt company called Threadless. Actually, to call it a T-shirt company is a bit of an understatement. In 2000, cofounders Jake Nickell and Jacob DeHart started the brand with just $1,000 in seed money and the revolutionary premise that employees and customers didn't have to be different groups of people.

Here's how Threadless does business: It asks its community of users (anyone can join for free) to submit their own shirt designs and then lets this community of users vote on which T-shirt designs are the best. The company gets as many as 300 submissions a day, but only makes 10 shirt designs from each week's submissions. Because the competition is so fierce, consumers who design shirts often email friends or post messages about the contest on their Facebook profiles to try to get votes—which helps them win *and* introduces new members into the Threadless community. The winning designs are then produced in get-it-while-it-lasts, limited-run

CONTINUES

CONTINUED

quantities for $20 each. The winning designer gets $2,000 cash, a $500 gift certificate to the site (which can be traded for $200 cash) and bragging rights. The company, meanwhile, spends *absolutely nothing* on advertising, has *absolutely no* paid sales force, and never produces a shirt that doesn't sell. Its dedicated community of users—who design, promote, vote on and ultimately buy the shirts—do almost everything for them (except for physically printing and shipping the shirts).

If that sounds like a fantastic business model, it is. Threadless boasts 1.6 million Twitter followers, 260,000 Facebook fans and sales figures that seem like they should be impossible for a company with just 60 employees. Threadless is privately held, so its financial data is not public, but *Forbes* reported that in 2009 the company brought in close to $30 million in revenue.[5]

While it might not be the first word that jumps to mind, Threadless is actually a classic customizer using the "customization lite" business model (which I described at greater length in chapter eight). It doesn't produce custom shirts for single individuals, but it does custom produce shirts for its coveted community on a totally made-to-order basis. Nothing is produced that hasn't already won the popularity contest, and by custom-making the shirts for the whole community, instead of for particular individuals, Threadless cashes in on something else individuals crave: the knowledge that their peers will like what they're wearing.

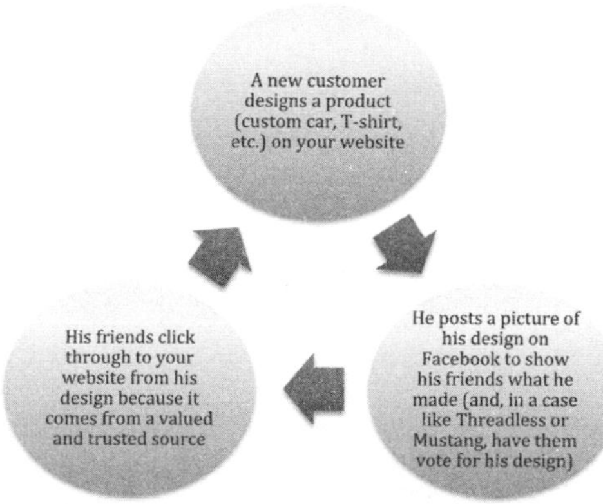

A new customer designs a product (custom car, T-shirt, etc.) on your website

He posts a picture of his design on Facebook to show his friends what he made (and, in a case like Threadless or Mustang, have them vote for his design)

His friends click through to your website from his design because it comes from a valued and trusted source

Figure 10.2   THE VIRTUOUS CYCLE OF CONSUMERS SHARING THEIR OWN DESIGNS

There is no business that wouldn't benefit from Threadless' perfect virtuous cycle, and excellent examples can already be found across extremely varied industries—from food to cars. Take Dunkin' Donuts, for example. In 2009 and 2010, the company ran contests to "Create Dunkin's Next Donut." Customers were invited to come to the website and mix and match doughnut shapes, icing, toppings, fillings and frostings to create a new doughnut and give it a great name. The contest's winning doughnut for each year was actually created and sold in stores for a limited time, and the winning designer won $12,000 and a trip to Dunkin's headquarters in Massachusetts.

At first glance this seems like classic "crowdsourcing," where companies look to customers to come up with ideas for new products, but the real payoff of the contest was the social media presence it got for Dunkin' Donuts. The company wasn't actually looking for a bestselling doughnut, as was evidenced by the fact that winning doughnuts were never slated to be sold for longer than a limited time in a limited number of locations. Here's what Dunkin' Donuts really got: a CIY bonanza with more than 500,000 doughnut creations,[6] which proud creators could SHARE with the click of a button with their friends via email, Facebook, LinkedIn, StumbleUpon, Twitter and a dozen other widely used social networking sites. In other words, Dunkin' Donuts didn't just get new doughnut ideas—it got a massive injection of social media buzz.

Sharing even works as a means of promotion when there are no winners, and the company simply custom produces every design its customers make and buy.

Rickshaw Bagworks, the custom messenger bag company that I discussed in chapter seven, has a "Fresh Bag Feed," which sends out pictures of the bags it produces as soon as they are finished to customers with Twitter accounts. Rickshaw founder and CEO Mark Dwight told us: "We tweet our customers a picture of a bag when it's on the factory floor. They're the designers [so] they feel really excited and want to share it."

Ford Mustang has secured a similar share mentality for consumers (even those who aren't buying cars, but just like designing them) by allowing them to easily share the cars they've created on a slew of social networking sites and enter their designs in head-to-head competitions with other amateur car creators.

Social media has also formed an integral part of YouBar's strategy for engaging with our customers. One element of this is our weekly photo contest, in which our customers send in pictures of themselves with their YouBars for the chance to win a free box of bars. The winner is decided by our Facebook fans, who vote (and comment) on the pictures. Another element of YouBar's social media presence is our daily Twitter tweets. Since YouBar doesn't have a brick-and-mortar storefront (the majority of customizers don't), social media ranks second only to our website as our most visible public face. I would love to say that I've personally presided over its development, but credit for that actually goes to my brother, Dennis Flynn, who is the director of marketing and social media at YouBar. He was the lead researcher for this book, and his ideas formed the basis of this entire chapter.

■ Pull Marketing

Dennis' take on the importance of social media is fascinating: He believes it is the natural epicenter of all marketing, advertising and promotion in the "post-traditional marketing world." In the 20th century, traditional (or push) marketing was born from the need to make a relatively small selection of mass-produced products appealing to everyone. One classic example comes from Dial, the soap company. In the mid-20th century, Dial became the richest soap brand in the United States by selling the idea that every single person in the entire country would benefit by using the same type of deodorant soap. Today it's hard to imagine any soap company selling the same soap to everyone. However, in 1953 Dial became famous for its enormously successful catchphrase, "Aren't you glad you use Dial? Don't you wish everybody did?"

By the end of the 20th century, consumers had become savvy to push marketing, and successful companies started pitching a more niche approach: making different types of products to target different types of consumers. Dial, for example, now has a line of body lotion called NutriSkin that comes in so many varieties that it has three different formulations for dry skin alone. Dennis believes that soon even this niche-based approach is going to be obsolete.

As Dennis puts it:

> At its core, push marketing involves a company deciding what's good for its bottom line and pushing that. We are now moving to what many people are calling a "pull marketing" approach, where the picture is reversed and consumers decide what they want, use online design tools to create it and then pull companies in to make it for them. Social media is the cornerstone of this because it is the place where a lot of this dialogue among the consumers, the consumers' valued peer groups and the producers take place.

"We are now moving to what many people are calling a 'pull marketing' approach, where the picture is reversed and consumers decide what they want, use online design tools to create it and then pull companies in to make it for them."

—Dennis Flynn, director of marketing and social media at YouBar

---

MASS PRODUCTION HAS ALWAYS BEEN WRONG FOR THE CONSUMER EXPERIENCE

By Andy Howell

Traditional marketing was born from the need to make appealing for the mass market the reduced selection that came out of mass production. The main message being sent was, "It's okay that everything is the same." Then, marketers attached fear ("You'll smell bad if you don't wear our deodorant!") and

CONTINUES

CONTINUED
celebrity endorsements. And there, in a nutshell, is the marketing philosophy for the entire 20th century. This process was great for a few people—it made them a lot of money—but it was bad for the majority of people. It trained consumers not to think for themselves, and not to create.

Now, thanks to the internet and the online design tools that we all have at our fingertips, that is changing. Creative people are going on websites like Zazzle and designing amazing stuff, not just for themselves but also to sell to small niche audiences of consumers who appreciate their aesthetic. I've met people making over $100,000 a year designing stationery on Zazzle. The creative person is empowered in the 21st century.

Andy Howell is the founder of Artsprojekt, a website offering customizable goods designed for artists (it is a subsidiary of Zazzle).

The Rules of Social Media Marketing for Customizers

I've alluded to the rules for establishing an excellent and organic presence on social media, but here, in more concise, reference-friendly form, are Dennis' three top rules for the new, pull marketing world of social media:

1. Give Your Customers Ownership of Their Designs Because Then They'll Want to Talk about Them

As companies like Threadless, Ford and Dunkin' Donuts demonstrate, there are multiple ways of giving customers creative ownership, but the core idea for all of them is to let your customers (either as a group or as individuals) customize their designs. Whether you as a company will produce every design customers create and purchase (like Rickshaw Bagworks) or just the winners (like Threadless) is a matter of preference and business model.

2. Make It Easy for Customers to Share What They've Designed

No matter how great your customers' creations are, if you don't make it easy for them to brag, you won't completely capitalize on the power consumers have to spread the word about your company. If you have a configurator on your website make sure to have a SHARE button that comes up when consumers are finished making their designs. The SHARE button should give them the ability to post the picture of their design to social networking sites like Facebook, Google+ and Twitter, and also let them email pictures of their designs directly to friends. This pays dividends: Websites that have sharing buttons for Twitter are linked to Twitter almost *seven times more often* than sites that don't have these SHARE buttons. In actual practice, this means that among the 10,000 largest websites, those that feature Twitter SHARE links boast roughly 27 tweets that include a link back to their own company sites, while those without Twitter SHARE buttons are mentioned in only four tweets that link back to their sites.[7]

In addition to these suggestions, it is ideal to encourage consumers to post a picture of their creations to your own site's gallery, where they can have their designs displayed and also browse others' creations. Galleries provide inspiration to customers and opportunities for design bragging rights, while simultaneously boosting your own website community.

In effect, the way "sharing" works online is like individual social interaction amplified. In fact, custom clothing manufacturer Made To Fit Me got its idea for a business from personal social interaction. Founder Alex Duncan had a friend whose mother had a few pieces of clothing made on a visit to Shanghai. When she got home and wore the pieces, her friends admired how beautiful they were and how well they fit. Made To Fit Me was born of the idea that everyone should be able to get clothes that fit that well. The company doesn't spend money on traditional marketing because it relies on powerful word-of-mouth marketing—both in person and online—to tell its story.

Online, though, is the real key. While a person might physically run into five or 10 friends that they tell the story of their clothes to, when they do it online, their recommendations are typically seen by many times that—as many as two or three *hundred* Facebook friends. Better still, because these friends are already online when they see the recommendation, the chances that they'll click through to your site goes way up.

One new company that is doing an excellent job of capitalizing on young consumers' desire to share their custom creations both online and in real life is CowCrowd. The Austria-based business allows users (the target market is 10- to 25-year-olds) the ability to create customized wooden necklace pendants, laser-engraved with the names of their friends, for just $5 each. Customers can share their designs on Facebook, through Cow-Crowd's own gallery and, of course, in person by *wearing* the necklaces. Paul Blazek, who started CowCrowd (he is also the founder and CEO of the configurator company cyLEDGE), told us, "These necklaces allow people to show their social networks in a simple, collectible, wearable way."

3. Be Present on the Right Social Networks

While there are still a few golden journalists and trendsetters that can create a megahit with a single sentence (think Oprah), for the most part the internet has created a world where the most trusted trendsetters are consumers' personal social networks and the niche blogs they read. It is vital to have active and vibrant profiles on all the social networking sites your target market uses. Facebook is the undeniable behemoth in this category, with 800 million users worldwide (defined as people who have logged in within the last 30 days). The record number of users for a single day reached the astounding number of *half a billion*.[8] No matter what type of company you have, you *must* be on Facebook.

Nielsen has done some research on which social networking sites are most important for companies to be present on. In a study that assessed the number of unique U.S. visitors that went to social networking sites during the month of May 2011, Nielsen found that Facebook was indeed the biggest by far, with 140 million unique U.S. visitors that month. But others were important too. With 24 million unique visitors per month, Twitter is definitely the second must-be-on social networking site.

In addition to these two biggies, there will probably be at least one or two other social networking sites that happen to be big with your particular demographic. WordPress, for example, which had 22 million monthly visitors as of May 2011, skews toward college-educated consumers (25 percent of its members have a bachelor's degree). Myspace, with 19 million unique visitors per month according to the Nielsen study, is particularly big with teenagers. LinkedIn, which showed 18 million unique visitors per month in the study, has three times more visitors with post-graduate degrees than other sites. Tumblr is popular with female teenagers, Yahoo! Pulse skews toward New Englanders and Wikia attracts the 18- to 34-year-old set.[9]

If your company has a global reach, remember that there are also key differences in which social networking websites are popular in different countries. In Brazil, Orkut is the biggest. In Japan, it's FC2 Blog. And in Britain, Tumblr is huge (although it is still second to Facebook).[10]

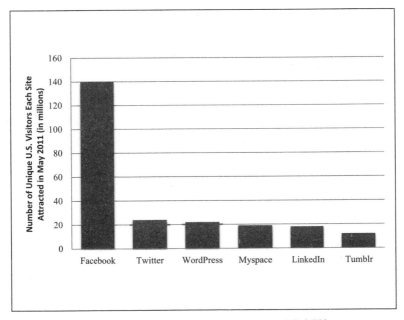

Figure 10.3 TOP U.S. SOCIAL NETWORKING WEBSITES

With social media being so new, however, there is constant change within the space, and giant new sites can arise quickly. Google+ was the social media website to watch—the site had more than 100 million users at the time of writing (although users still weren't spending more than an average of three minutes a month on the site). The idea here is to do some online research before launching your social media presence to ensure that you aren't overlooking the latest phenomenon. Most importantly, make sure to establish the favorite social media site of your target demographic. It may not have made this chart because it is relatively small by comparison, but if all your target customers are on it, it could be huge for you. Care2, for example, is a social networking site that is very popular with environmentalists. So, any business with a green angle should make sure to have a presence on the site. After launching your business, keep checking which social media sites are emerging to make sure you're on board with relevant ones early.

For more up-to-date information about how to customize your marketing, including the latest information about the most popular social networking sites for your company's target demographic, visit CustomNation.com/Marketing.

For more information about the companies discussed throughout this book, visit Custom Nation.com/Companies.

CHAPTER 11

Keep Growing Your CIY Business

I like to think about this as the "*after* the happily ever after" chapter (which is why I think it belongs here at the end of the book). It is for the period of time *after* you've already become a moderate success: You have a loyal following of customers, new ones are coming through your virtual door every day and you're getting enough press that friends and family have even seen your company in the news or on TV. I knew I'd hit this moment when I was out at my local bar one night. It was about a year after I'd launched YouBar, and I still hadn't perfected the sound bite of what I did for a living when I was out meeting new people. I would say something like, "I make custom nutrition bars." And the person wouldn't understand what I was talking about and would go talk to someone else.

But that night—soon after YouBar had been covered by Fox and in *The New York Times*—all that changed. I met some of my friend's friends at the bar, and they asked me what I did. I gave my usual awkward reply and—shockingly—two of them said, "Are you Anthony Flynn?" When I said, "Yes," they said, "We love your bars! That's so cool!"

Things feel so good in this late-beginning period of running a company that it can be tempting to glide; but to keep doing well, it's vital to keep *continued growth* at the front of your mind. So I've compiled a list of the 10 big ideas that are important *after* the initial flush of success in order to keep growing.

1. Bring Material and Shipping Costs Down, and Keep On Doing It

When you first start out, the amount of materials you need and the number of shipments you make will inevitably be small, so you'll be paying over-the-counter style prices. As your sales grow, it's important to renegotiate deals with your shippers *every quarter* and your suppliers *every time you place a large order* to keep bringing your wholesale prices down. Lots of business people either forget to do this or don't realize how important it is, and so they aren't paying as little as they could. I spoke to the CEO of one large company that ships more than double the amount of product You-Bar ships but is paying considerably more per package in shipping charges because he hasn't renegotiated terms with the company's shipping company often enough.

Not every negotiation will bring your prices down, but sometimes it will, and at the very least, you will likely get some helpful recommendations. For example, your shipping company will have detailed data on exactly how much you send to exactly which places, and it might have recommendations on how to bundle or reorganize your shipments to make your costs less even without a further discount. This type of cost-cutting is especially important for customizers because we ship directly to customers' homes and therefore don't typically benefit from the discounted prices companies offer for sending large shipments to single locations like retail stores.

When you're first starting out, make sure to open an account with your shipping company, or companies. FedEx and UPS both offer substantial discounts simply for having an account with them, even if you aren't shipping high volumes of product. They sometimes will also offer those with accounts useful technology, like shipping label makers, free labels, computers with integrated scales and pickups directly from your facility.

GETTING THE MOST OUT OF YOUR SHIPPING COMPANY

When you need help the most—in the very beginning—it's basically impossible to catch any breaks. Shipping companies have scant deals for startups, and how, you might wonder, can you compete with the big guys if you can't get good rates from them? But if you stick to your business plan, the breakthrough point happens sooner than you'd probably expect. For YouBar, the breakthrough point for shipping costs was when we started shipping $50,000 a year in goods. When this happens, shipping companies will start falling over themselves to make you happy. I won't deny that I've enjoyed some perks, but far and away the best benefits of all when you open the door to this new kind of relationship are the deals you'll get on cost and the machines they'll give you.

When I first started YouBar, we had to take every customer's address from PayPal and manually cut and paste it (or retype it) into the UPS or FedEx address format in order to make the shipment. However, when our volume increased, FedEx gave us free software to cut out all this work. Now, we take every order that comes in for the whole week, upload it into FedEx's "shipping manager" software program, and the software instantly prints out all the shipping labels for every order. Not only does this eliminate the need for us to retype address information, the software also automatically recognizes what shipping speed each customer chose and how much weight each shipment will be. To give you a sense of how much this automation has saved YouBar, in 2007 we had one full-time person dedicated to shipping. Now—with 10 times more sales—we still have just one full-time person dedicated to our shipping. In effect, we have lowered our shipping labor costs tenfold.

■ 2. Don't Take No for an Answer . . .

When working with your suppliers, co-packers or shippers in the world of customization, it is almost certain that you will hear the phrase "we can't do that" relatively often. Because most businesses are still operating with a mass-production mind-set, custom ideas can be challenging. But, as I hope I've effectively shown you throughout this book, it is possible to mass customize almost anything in the modern world, and it is your job to spark imaginative solutions to the complicated customizing questions that will naturally arise. Often this means long, creative conversations that promote out-of-the-box thinking.

Matt Lauzon from Gemvara, the jeweler we profiled in chapter four, told us that he had to convince a lot of his jewelry suppliers that making their jewelry to order was financially viable. "The only reason we can do what we do," he said, "is that we [persuaded] pretty big, longstanding jewelry-manufacturing companies to completely reorganize to support us."

Because he put that energy into starting the relationship, the ongoing connection is great. "We view it that we are their customer [just as much as] they are our customer," Matt said. This has paid off for everyone. When sales soared during 2011, and Matt suddenly needed more office space, one of his suppliers even let the company move in with them. "That's the kind of relationship we have," he said.

■ 3. . . . But Do Learn to *Say* No

It can be hard to say no to business when you are still relatively new to the game, especially when you pride yourself on being able to deliver custom solutions. But there are going to be times when you have to weigh the costs and the risks. At YouBar, for example, we've had requests for bars made with "food-grade crickets" or medicinal marijuana that we had to politely decline because of the reputational risks those ingredients would create. We also initially had to say no to requests for extra-large nutrition bars because of the significant costs associated with adding a new size of package. (We now offer extra-large bars, but we only started doing that after we knew there was high enough demand to warrant the extra costs). In a similar vein, Zazzle spends a lot making sure it says no to any consumers that make designs that violate copyright and publicity rights. To that end, Zazzle employs an entire team of reviewers whose sole job is to ensure that no copyright-infringing designs—like Mickey Mouse flashing the middle finger—ever make it to production. Ultimately, Zazzle's reviewers reject roughly 5 percent of orders the company receives on this basis.

At YouBar, for example, we've had requests for bars made with "food-grade crickets" or medicinal marijuana that we had to politely decline because of the reputational risks those ingredients would create.

It's not just customers that you have to learn to say "no" to in some instances. Once you start getting a lot of press, you'll get calls from an increasing number of people—most of whom simply aren't serious business people—who claim that they have the clout and resources to make giant orders. They'll often call up with big claims, like saying that they have a website that gets a million hits a day. Thankfully, in the internet world, it's easy to check their veracity. Google rankings don't lie. My rule of thumb, however, is pretty simple. Typically, the people who want to take up the most of your time (meet you in person, come to your production facility, etc.) are the least serious. The biggest deals that we get are usually also the most straightforward and involve zero face time. We've closed deals for as many as 100,000 bars simply through email.

◼ 4. Let Go to Let Grow

Customizing is usually a fairly labor-intensive business model. Each product is made for clients specifically to order, and so when you're first starting out in the business, it's typical that you'll spend a fair amount of time putting your own labor into making the products you sell. When I first started YouBar, my cofounder and I made every single bar we shipped, and we did all the customer service. As we started getting more orders, we had to hire staff to make the bars, provide customer service and organize shipping. At first I found it difficult to let go of doing everything. I remember tasting every single recipe our first employee made before shipping it out, long after she had perfected her bar-making skills.

The problem was that not letting go meant I didn't have the time to put into seeking new ingredient suppliers, making shipping more efficient and cost-effective, connecting with the press (online and off) and planning longer-term expansion. When I finally started delegating responsibilities—and stopped going into the kitchen every day—growth came much more naturally. I was able to focus on long-term growth while our excellent kitchen manager, Jimmy Castaneda, took care of all the day-to-day production.

> When I finally started delegating responsibilities—and stopped going into the kitchen every day—growth came much more naturally.

I have a friend who runs a successful restaurant in Los Angeles, which is often frequented by celebrities (because of that, he asked not to be quoted by name). Recently, he expanded into private catering. When I marveled about how busy he must be, he looked at me with incredibly relaxed eyes. He said, "You know, because I'm now doing the catering and the restaurant, I can't be everywhere, and I've had to start trusting my staff more. The funny thing is that the more I sit back, the better the business does! Now that my business is booming more than ever, I'm doing less work than ever before."

5. Launch a Great Configurator (the Website Tool That Allows Customers to Create Beautiful, Visually Rich Custom Products Online)

At the point that you have a fairly substantial amount of money to dedicate to a top-of-the-line custom website, it makes sense to contact one of the companies that specialize in this. Currently, Fluid is the frontrunner for this in the United States, although it typically takes contracts for large, established companies, like Reebok, and charges in excess of $100,000. We did, however, speak to Fluid's VP of product engineering, Andrew Guldman, to get a sense of what configurators can bring to the table. "It creates a good user experience [that is] fun, playful and interactive," Andrew said.

To obtain a good configurator for less money, try Treehouse Logic, which has developed a proprietary platform that gives customers the ability to build a configurator for a fraction of the price, usually starting around $10,000. Treehouse Logic's CEO Dave Sloan told my coauthor that with companies like Fluid "building a configurator [is] a service; it's like hiring a lawyer" for a per-hour charge.

Dave said, "Our approach is the opposite. We have a configurator-building tool. You can build it however you want." As a result, costs to the customer plummet by as much as tenfold.

Want to spend less than $10,000? I have several ideas for this in chapter seven, but even getting a full-fledged configurator may soon be attainable for next-to-nothing up front. As we outlined in depth in that chapter, there is an exciting group of companies in Europe that is working on creating a similar platform to the one Treehouse Logic has, but this new platform will be free for you to put on your website, and will make money by charging you a percentage of sales to use it. Klaus Pilsl, the technical mastermind behind this new platform, which is called Combeenation, told me that Combeenation's engine is already working, with beta testing scheduled to begin in mid-2012 and full-scale rollout slated for 2013. "This is a big leap forward," Klaus told me excitedly. If it delivers what is promised, it will make configurators affordable for every single business, no matter how small.

INVESTING IN TECHNOLOGY

Once you get big enough to invest in technology, your website shouldn't be the only place you look. All the biggest and best customizing companies have invested heavily in incredible new technology to make customization on a large scale financially competitive with mass production. Examples can be found in every industry—from jewelers, like Blue Nile and Gemvara, to sneaker companies, like Nike and Adidas. CafePress, for example, was among the first digital on-demand companies to start printing on dark T-shirts digitally, beginning in 2005. Since then it has innovated dozens of additional revolutionary printing methods to enable high-quality custom printing on everything from camcorders to aluminum water bottles.

■6. Write a Blog

If you don't have one already, it is worth launching a blog on your site that broadcasts news relevant to your topic. At YouBar, we have a health and fitness blog that we try to add new entries to at least once a week. The blog is a great way of fostering a bond with your customers and a community feeling on your website. In addition, when potential customers use search engines like Google, your blog, if relevant, could bring new customers to your website.

■7. Hold Monthly Wish-List Meetings

Sometimes, when things are going well, it can be easy to get complacent—a recipe for eventual decline. One fun way to prevent this is to hold regular "wish-list meetings" with top staff members. These are a great way of generating new ideas and identifying solutions to production bottlenecks. During one such meeting at YouBar in our second year, we discussed the problem we were having with customers requesting bars with professional bodybuilder levels of protein powder. So much protein powder made the bars dry, and well, powdery. The question on the table was: What could we do to deliver the custom ingredients while still making a delicious product? And that is how our custom protein shake business was born.

■8. Think about Going Global

In terms of the number of customizing companies it hosts, the United States is the global leader with 58 percent of the world's total number of such companies. Germany is next with 28 percent, followed by the rest of Western Europe with 12 percent. In total, this means that 98 percent of the world's customizing companies are located in the United States and Western Europe. The potential for global growth in customizing is immense. As a result, many established customizers are selling beyond their borders. Germany's mymuesli, which launched in 2007, now ships to four other countries across Europe—Austria, Switzerland, the United Kingdom and the Netherlands.

Zazzle is likewise seeing enormous growth from its increased internationalization. The company, which launched its U.S.-only website in 2005, now hosts 17 international sites and ships to 224 countries. In 2008, just 3 percent of Zazzle's revenue came from outside of the United States. By 2011 that number had climbed to 20 percent, with the company anticipating global demand to account for half of its sales eventually. "We're seeing interest in custom content from every part of the globe," Zazzle cofounder Jeff Beaver told us.[1]

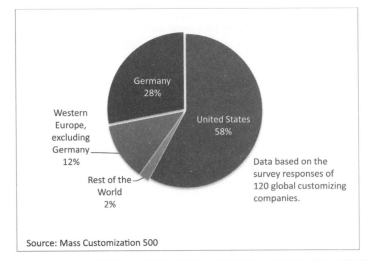

Data based on the survey responses of 120 global customizing companies.

Source: Mass Customization 500

Figure 11.1 PERCENTAGE OF CUSTOMIZING COMPANIES IN EACH GLOBAL REGION

In addition, for long-term company growth, it is important for any online company to keep an eye on the global market, as the vast majority of internet users in the world simply aren't in North America. See Figure 11.2.

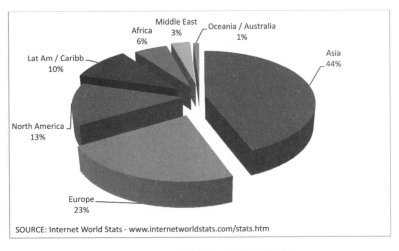

SOURCE: Internet World Stats - www.internetworldstats.com/stats.htm

Figure 11.2 INTERNET USERS IN THE WORLD, DISTRIBUTION BY WORLD REGIONS—2011

A WORD OF WARNING ON GOING GLOBAL

When you decide to expand internationally, Jeffrey Housenbold, the CEO of Shutterfly and a former top executive at eBay, said it's extremely important to launch a site that will speak clearly to your new geographical market. "When we launched eBay UK," he said, "we first launched it in American English, not the Queen's English, and it suffered. You have to not only do it, but do it right."

9. Consider Getting Outside Investment to Fund Fast Expansion

At some point—typically when sales have passed $1 million a year—it is wise to consider whether you might want to attract angel investors or venture capitalists to fund the next level of expansion. Many business owners choose not to do this—sometimes taking out loans instead—as it inevitably means selling off a large portion of their company and no longer being the sole owner. However, if you do think this downside is worth the upside of potentially supersonic expansion and valuable expertise, many VCs are now eagerly looking at customizing companies for investment opportunities.

Josh Elman, a principal at venture capital firm Greylock Partners, which has $1 billion in capital and has invested in giants like Facebook and Pandora, said that "public markets are now valuing customization, [and] personalization is disrupting many long-standing industries," leading his firm to look carefully at customizing companies with what he calls "billion-plus potential." (If Josh sounds familiar, I also quoted him in chapter two).

While researching this book, my coauthor and I asked Josh how a new entrepreneur could get funding from a company like his, and here's what he told us:

> The pithy answer is build a great product you're excited about. Once you've done that investors are going to want to be there.

The most important thing isn't a level [of sales or profit], but a rhythm that can then be repeated like a great big flywheel. Zazzle is a great example. It's a designer marketplace. The engine feeds on itself.

Gemvara's Matt Lauzon, who has secured more than $51 million in VC and angel investor funding for his company, had advice for this book too. "Don't claim to have all the answers" when you speak to potential investors, he told us. "Build relationships. Prove as much as you can. Mitigate risk. And get them to trust that you can get the right team."

■ 10. Pursue Big Orders

The majority of this book has focused on the business of customizing for individual consumers, but companies also require tailor-made goods for their employees, trade shows and events, like movie premieres. These types of orders are typically called co-packing (in the food industry) or wholesaling (in other industries), and most customizing companies actively pursue them. One great example of successful wholesaling is Skinit, the custom computer case company, which has deals with HP and Microsoft. At You-Bar, our first larger orders were from personal trainers and dieticians who wanted to sell nutrition bars to their clients under their own labels that were tailor-made to fit their nutritional ethos.

Although profit margins are lower on larger orders, producing larger amounts can push a company to create new processes and techniques that achieve economies of scale so that your cost per unit goes down. Larger orders can also help spread out your revenue more evenly throughout the year (e.g., beyond the busy Christmas season).

CafePress has merchandising deals with some of the world's biggest movie franchises, like the *Twilight* series and *The Hunger Games*. These licensing deals allow movie fans to go on CafePress' website and create and sell merchandise around their favorite characters and catchphrases.

One popular *Twilight*-based design, for example, was simply a T-shirt that read "Cullen Baseball." (The Cullens are the fictional vampire family featured in the movie.) Such fan merchandising is a win-win-win situation. Fans get unique, inside joke–based gear they love, movie studios get merchandising revenues without having to pay designers, and the customizers that do the production get big orders thanks to the large number of fans these movie franchises boast.

For regular, up-to-date blogs on how to keep growing your custom business, go to CustomNation.com.

For more information about the companies discussed throughout this book, visit CustomNation.com/Companies.

Afterword

Customizing Your Food for a Perfect Body and Great Health

When I first conceived of this book, I actually wanted to write a book on the ways that the booming business of food customization will help Americans live longer, lose weight and express themselves like never before. As the book took shape and found a publisher, however, it became clear that the health and fitness side of customization simply didn't fit with the main text of the business book that was taking form.

That being said, the health and fitness appeal of food customizing is incredible; it is what led me to my business originally, and I thought it would be of interest to any readers with a passion for personal health and fitness. Because this afterword is so personal to me, I thought it made sense to start with the personal anecdote of how the desire to customize my food inspired me to start YouBar. . . .

It was the winter of 2006. I had just graduated from USC with a business degree and while figuring out what to do next, I started teaching snowboarding with my mom, who has been teaching since 1998. On our long drives to and from work at the mountain, one of our favorite topics of discussion was nutrition. We're both extremely health-conscious, so the latest *Science* magazine study or hottest must-eat fruit were conversational staples. But there was one food discussion that we kept coming back to, not because we enjoyed it but because it annoyed both of us so much.

As snowboard instructors, stopping to eat lunch was never something we wanted to do. Either we were teaching or we were boarding. So, like a lot of athletes, we liked to eat pocket-portable energy bars for lunch. The problem was that all the energy bars on the shelves back then had something wrong with them. They had things like high-fructose corn syrup, preservatives and/or lots of ingredients we didn't want. Why hadn't anyone made the perfect bar? We started talking about what that would be, and immediately realized the problem. Our "perfect bars" were as different as could be. I wanted higher protein and higher fat; she wanted moderate protein and less sugar. Flavor was also a point of contention: I hate peanut butter; my mom loves it.

So, we gave up on the idea of a single "perfect bar" and started hand-making our own perfect bars from scratch. Mine were packed with fresh dates and raw almonds. My mom's had peanut butter, cocoa powder and whey protein. Within a few weeks of ditching my mass-produced bars, something really cool happened: I felt better.

I hadn't quite realized I'd felt bad before, but getting rid of the foods I knew didn't agree with me (like preservatives and whey protein) made an enormous difference. I shaved 20 minutes off my marathon time, I landed a jump 180 in the snowboard park for the first time and my stamina skyrocketed: After six hours of teaching, I was able to freeride for another three hours. I wasn't trying to lose weight, but I dropped 20 pounds. My mom was feeling just as great. So one day on our way down from the mountain, we finally had the conversation that had been obvious for months. "There is such a thing as the perfect bar," I said. "I know," she replied. "It's just different for everyone." And the rest is history.

■ Live Longer

My experience is a classic example of something that the strongest biological research today is showing: If we don't eat the right foods for our individual bodies, we're doomed to develop thick waistlines, feel lethargic and ultimately develop the chronic killer diseases, like heart disease and diabetes, that are linked to obesity and sedentary lifestyles. So how do we know what's right for us to eat? For many of us, we simply *feel* better with certain foods. But scientists are starting to decode this feeling and quantify it. It turns out, it's actually all in our genes.

Scientists believe that within the next decade doctors will have the genetic tools to customize diets for their individual patients. Right now, doctors already do this to a limited extent. As anyone who has ever been to a general checkup knows, doctors take medical histories of diseases your parents/grandparents/siblings have suffered from and make broad brushstroke dietary recommendations accordingly. Is heart disease common in your family? Avoid red meat. Is diabetes prevalent? Limit sugars.

And these recommendations promise to get much better soon. Many scientists believe that by the year 2020, doctors will be able to map their patients' entire genomes as easily as they currently analyze a urine sample. By taking a DNA sample (a strand of hair or a swab of saliva), your doctor will be able to determine exactly what diseases you are most at risk of developing and create a customized nutrition plan accordingly.

When the human genome was first mapped in 2003, it took 15 years and cost nearly $3 billion to do it. But since then, gene-mapping technology has taken off. Today companies like Complete Genomics will sequence your genome for just $5,000 in less than a month. Academics widely predict that by 2013, you'll be able to get your genome mapped for $1,000 in 24 hours. And by 2020, it'll be as standard as a blood test.

Once doctors have your genome in hand, they'll be able to cross-reference the diseases lurking menacingly in your genes with the scientific knowledge of what types of diets stop those diseases from manifesting and create a customized eating plan accordingly. The burgeoning science that looks at this detailed link between genes and diet is called nutritional genomics, or "nutrigenomics." So, when my coauthor and I were researching this afterword, we spoke to Raymond Rodriguez, the head of the Center of Excellence for Nutritional Genomics at the University of California, Davis.

"The genotype is what makes you completely unique," Raymond told us. "But what we're discovering is that superimposed on the genotype is the environmental interaction." What we eat can actually "reprogram" our gene activity. This calls into question everything we thought we knew about our genes.

Since scientists first discovered DNA in the 1940s, we have been inclined to think of genes as destiny. People with so-called "bad genes" were doomed to die young of whatever disease was written in their DNA. We thought eating "good foods" could put off the inevitable and give a person a few extra years, and that "bad foods" might accelerate the disease, but ultimately a person's genetic destiny was locked from birth.

Nutrigenomics flips this picture on its head; scientists now see the relationship between genes and diet as an ongoing dialogue. Certain foods can enhance the power of protective genes, while others can suppress them. At the same time, other foods can "turn on" or "turn off" bad genes. In other words, food works together with genes to determine our destiny, *not* genes alone.

This supports what we all know anecdotally. A few people, like Winston Churchill, can subsist on cigars and champagne and still live to 90. But the vast majority of people clearly live (and die) according to a combination of genes and diet. Take, for example, Indian women. In India, only 1 in 40 women develop breast cancer. But in the United States, 1 out of every 8 ethnically Indian women gets the disease.[1] Genetically, these women are the same. So what accounts for the *fivefold* difference? Researchers believe it is predominantly the result of diet.

Indian women in the United States generally eat a diet high in saturated fat, which promotes the development of breast cancer. At the same time, they typically eat less of one of the most common Indian spices, which is known to cut breast cancer risk: turmeric. In the future, when we all have our genes mapped, women of Indian ethnicity will know whether they have this roughly 1 in 5 genetic predisposition to breast cancer and will be able to modify their diets to prevent the cancer from manifesting by eating, for example, less saturated fat and more turmeric.

Right now, that particular future is still a distance off because we don't know exactly which gene, or combination of genes, are responsible for Indian women's predisposition to breast cancer. But we are already at the point of being able to make specific dietary recommendations relating to other genes. One stellar example: the gene for a protein known as Apo E, which helps regulate cholesterol. This gene comes in three variants—e2, e3 and e4 (e3 is the most common). People with the e2 variant are lucky—they typically have lower-than-average cholesterol. But the e4 variant—which an estimated 15 percent to 30 percent of the population possesses—can be deadly. It dramatically increases the risk of diabetes, raises cholesterol levels and makes the risk of smoking-related heart disease soar. If a person with the e4 variant smokes, he is almost certain to get heart disease; if he's overweight, he is almost certain to develop diabetes. However, e4 responds dramatically to environmental factors, like diet. If a person with the e4 variant eats a diet low in saturated fat, exercises, doesn't smoke and doesn't drink, he can remove *all* the genetic predisposition for heart disease and diabetes that come with e4.

When we all have our genomes mapped, we'll know if we carry e4 and be able to make the dietary changes necessary to combat the risks that gene variant poses. Of course, eating low-fat food and not smoking would be good for everyone. But with gene testing, diets are specialized for us, erasing our all-too-easy ability to believe that maybe we, too, are one of the lucky few who can subsist on cigars and champagne and live to 90 like Churchill.

GREAT TASTE MEETS GREAT HEALTH: THE VEGGIE GRILL

One of the biggest problems with nutritional genomics, say nay-sayers, is its lack of foodie fun. Say you love steak, but your nutritional genome says you have to be a veggie-tastic vegan. Well, a growing number of smart entrepreneurs are launching businesses to address this exact issue. Food scientists have already perfected artificial flavors (think Jelly Belly jelly beans); now top chefs and fancy food processors are perfecting artificial textures. That means a delicious authentic-tasting steak can be concocted from broccoli and soy protein. In other words, you can have your steak and eat it too.

Consider the Veggie Grill, a booming California restaurant chain that serves American comfort food . . . with a catch. All of Veggie Grill's food—including chicken wings, steak sandwiches, nachos and fries—is made from completely vegan ingredients. I met Veggie Grill's founder, T.K. Pillan, when we were both invited to speak at a conference at UCLA's Anderson School of Management. I've been a huge fan of Veggie Grill since the day it first opened back in 2006, and I asked him what inspired him. He told me that the idea of the grill was, "To get past the stereotype of the vegetarian place. . . . We've shocked some customers when they found out that the great steak sandwich they just ate was actually a veggie protein blend."

■ Lose Weight

This kind of detailed understanding of specific gene interactions is also where some of the most promising research related to weight loss is coming from. Forget the low-carb/low-fat debate. It turns out that there is no single right answer; all of us have genes that *either* respond better to a low-fat diet or a low-carbohydrate diet. Early research indicates that if you really want to lose weight, you need to know which you have and customize your diet accordingly.

The best study to date proving this came out of Stanford University, which found that—among the 141 subjects used in the study—those with a genetic predisposition to low-carb eating (determined by a simple saliva DNA test) *lost between two and three times more weight* when on a low-carb diet, such as Atkins, than those on the same diet without the predisposition. Similar results were true in the opposite direction: Those with low-fat genotypes lost significantly more weight on low-fat diets, like the Ornish diet, than those without that genotype.[2] The right diet, in other words, means the difference between losing 10 pounds and losing 25 pounds. The results were so stunning that they made the front page of *The Wall Street Journal* when they were published.

I was so fascinated by the study that I called up the company that Stanford sourced its test from, Massachusetts-based Interleukin Genetics Inc., to take the test myself. They sent me a simple cheek-swab test that I mailed back to them. Two weeks later I got the results: My genes say I need a low-fat diet and high-intensity workouts to keep in shape. These findings coincided exactly with what I already knew about my body based on my experience with different foods and exercise. They confirmed that the diet I follow (a modified form of the Paleo Diet) and the high-intensity Cross-Fit workout that I do five days a week are perfectly tailored to my individual genetic footprint. My personalized Paleo/CrossFit regime has led me to great health: I'm 6 feet 1 inch tall, 175 pounds, bench 210 pounds and run a mile in 5 minutes and 29 seconds.

Lew Bender, the CEO of Interleukin, is scientific when he talks about the gene test. "Fatty acid–binding protein 2 is one of the genes we look at," he said. "People who have a variant of this gene absorb three times as much fat as people without this gene variation, and so typically, unless they have other genes to balance it out, need to reduce the amount of fat in their diets. What our genetic test does is give you a clear and understandable idea of how best to lose weight as an individual."

When I asked Lew what he thought the biggest benefit of the test was in practical terms, he said: "Right now, the vast majority of people play diet roulette. This test lets you end that cycle by giving you insight into whether your genes mean that you more efficiently use carbs or fat from food and also how your genes help your body better metabolize those nutrients." Lew, incidentally, is a rare "balancer" (a genetic type that about 16 percent of the population possesses), which means he doesn't just need to cut carbs or cut fat; rather, he needs a specific ratio of fat and carbs to maintain a healthy figure.

Interleukin's test is a genetic means of learning about your individual food needs, but the company is certainly not alone in believing that food should be personalized. At YouBar, for example, we make nutrition bars for thousands of personal trainers, dieticians and nutritionists—all of whom tailor the nutrients in their bars for their clients' precise dietary and exercise regimens—deciding everything from the number of calories per bar to the amount of protein per bar. Some of these nutritionists also include what we call "infusions" in their clients' bars—these are extra additions of vitamins (such as vitamin C and calcium), fiber and omega-3 fatty acids to match their clients' exact health needs.

As an interesting side note to this: There are also a growing number of companies, including 23andMe (which was named one of *Time*'s "Best Inventions of 2008"), Gene Link, Garden State Nutritionals and MyGeneWize, which also take DNA samples from their clients (none of these companies do full genotype maps yet). Then, they analyze these samples to produce customized advice, vitamin packs or protein powders that can decrease personal health risks and make up for individual deficiencies. The industry is not, however, regulated by the Food and Drug Administration yet, so before using any of these, it is wise to do research and consult your doctor.

■ Express Yourself

In addition to giving us good long-term health and fit bodies, custom food also feeds another important human hunger: self-expression. There was a time when, "What's your sign?" was the catchall, get-to-know-you phrase.

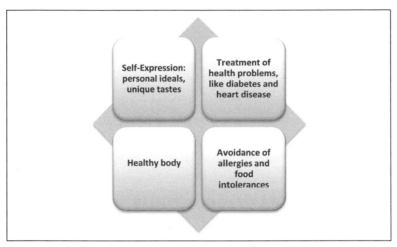

Figure A.1   REASONS CONSUMERS WANT CUSTOM FOOD

Today, it's arguably been replaced by, "What's your food?" We express complex belief systems by subscribing to food movements like "slow" and "freegan." We take political stances on "organic," "local" and "genetically modified" foods. We express concern for the welfare of humanity, animals and the environment by eating "fair trade," "free range" and "sustainable." Customizing our food and getting involved in the creative process behind it is a key method that we use to tell others (and ourselves) who we are.

One of my favorite examples of a customizing company that feeds the intellectual hunger for custom food and drink is Sonoma Valley–based wine customizer, Crushpad. Michael Brill, Crushpad's founder, has given the creative side of customization a lot of thought. And here's what he has to say about it:

> As people accumulate more wealth, they get to the point where they've already bought all the stuff they need and are bored of buying things. People want to express themselves through creating things, and making wine is a unique way to express who you are in our new experience economy.

> Our clients are really telling a story about themselves when they make their wines. They select which vineyard their grapes come from, based on the style of wine they want to create, and they can

even go and pick the grapes themselves. We have clients from across the world that fly in to our winery on the day of the harvest and can participate in any part of the winemaking process over the course of a wine's two-year development—from fermentation to design to bottling. Our clients get to live out the good parts of a winemaker's life without the exhaustion that comes from months of 14-hour days of grueling labor. There simply is no replacement for the feeling you get when you share a bottle of wine that you took from an idea to a finished bottle.

■The Business Opportunity

It almost goes without saying, but there is a lot of money to be made from Americans' hunger for custom food and drink. Based on the number of wines Crushpad has helped its customers create, for example, I estimate that the company has had roughly $40 million in revenue since launching in 2004. It isn't the only one. Since 2004 America has witnessed an explosion in the number of food and drink companies with custom business models. As recently as 2008 there were fewer than 10 companies that sold fully customizable food and drinks. Today, there are more than 120 such companies, customizing such things as chocolate, cereal, trail mix, tea, beef jerky, beer and even pet food.

The world's biggest food producers—including Mars, Heineken, Frito-Lay, Coca-Cola and Ben & Jerry's—are also starting to customize. These established brands aren't getting rid of mass production, of course. They're still selling millions of bags of Fritos and millions of cases of Coke. But, at the same time, they are enticing consumers with exciting new elements of CIY—like personalized labels, high levels of consumer input in creating new product lines and fun online design tools.

If you start looking for it, you'll see examples everywhere. Heineken allows its European customers to customize six-packs of beer with completely personalized labels (the United States has rules against selling alcohol online). Mars, the snack maker, lets customers put their own names, photos or logos directly on M&M's. Ben & Jerry's and Frito-Lay have both run extensive campaigns asking their customers to design new flavors of ice cream and potato chips for them. The list goes on and on.

Importantly, however, there is still an enormous amount of space in the custom food and drink industries for smart new entrepreneurs to fill. Food companies that customize for their clients capitalize on dozens of markets, including the $60 billion-a-year diet industry, the $26 billion market for those with allergies and other intolerances and the *booming* baby boomer health food market. We are long past the age of a one-size-fits-all diet.

■The $60 Billion-a-Year Diet Industry

In the 1950s the American diet industry was estimated to be worth just $100 million a year. By 1990 it had grown to $20 billion a year. Since then it has tripled to $60 billion annually. Back in the 1950s, all the diets available were versions of low-calorie: most famously, the Grapefruit Diet and the Cabbage Soup Diet. Since then the types of diets have multiplied exponentially. Notable household names include Atkins, South Beach, the Zone and Master Cleanse. Every year, publishers come out with hundreds of new diet titles.

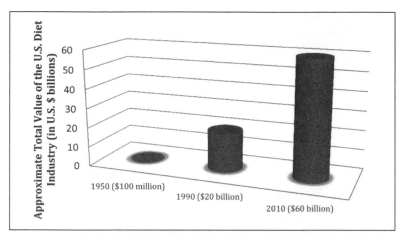

Figure A.2   THE U.S. DIET INDUSTRY
Source: Data from Columbia University Graduate School of Journalism (masters project), "Body iCon," by Kim Dixon, Tiffany Kary and Dan Maccarone, published in 1999; *Chicago Tribune*, "Resolutions Still Carry Weight At This Wee Time Of The Year," by Barbara Mahany (Jan 8, 1986); and *The New York Times*, "Diet Companies Promote New Ways to Reduce," by Elizabeth Olson, (Jan 6, 2011)

A growing number of doctors and nutritionists are embracing food individualism and drawing fascinating links between individual health needs and genetic predisposition to disease and how nutrition can prevent some illnesses from developing or progressing. Many books in this genre have even become runaway bestsellers, including *Eat Right for Your Type* and *YOU: On a Diet.*

While it's fashionable to mock the industry, knowledge about nutrition feeds a real hunger: There are 310 million people living in the United States and there simply isn't a single diet that will satisfy everyone. A Google search for the phrase "custom diet" turns up 93 million results. (Incidentally, when I first looked up that statistic in 2010, "custom diet" only turned up 52 million results.)

Food producers that embrace this fact—and allow their products to be customized to suit different types of diets—are able to capture a much wider potential market than those relying on one-diet-fits-all, mass-produced recipes.

The $26 Billion-a-Year Allergy and Intolerance Market

The global market for products targeted at people who suffer from food allergies and intolerances is growing faster than the types of gluten-free pasta on store shelves. Large supermarkets now have whole sections devoted to "Free From" ranges, teeming with products that are gluten-free, milk-free, casein-free, egg-free, wheat-free, soy-free and, of course, nut-free. But that's only the tip of the iceberg. Every year there are a growing number of cases of children being born with allergies to everything from strawberries to salmon. Today 3 percent to 5 percent of the U.S. population is allergic to milk, eggs, peanuts, tree nuts or seafood.[3] And top allergists all agree that this number is on the rise, although the reasons for the increase still aren't understood. Global Industry Analysts, a leading business think tank, estimates that the market for foods that cater to people with allergies and intolerances will *surpass $26 billion a year by 2017.*[4]

The opportunity for food customizers is obvious. Companies that make customized food can satisfy the hunger of the growing population of people with allergies and intolerances by tailoring each product to suit each consumer's needs. Better still, food customizers appeal to both people with the most common allergies (as represented in supermarkets' "free-from" aisles) *and* people suffering from the least common allergies or difficult allergy combinations (such as an allergy to wheat, nuts *and* milk), who currently often have no option other than to prepare their own food at home.

The Baby Boomer Market: Eating Up $39 Billion a Year of 'Functional Foods'

Baby boomers have been hit by a double financial whammy: They're hitting 65 and are supposed to be retiring, but their retirement savings (if they had any in the first place) have been wiped out by the recent global economic downturn. So, having lost their jobs *and* their savings, they're cutting back on spending, leading smart brand managers and marketers to start widening their nets to target younger consumers (as I outlined in the previous chapter). There is, however, one exception to boomers' belt-tightening: their health.

Boomers' golden years haven't just come with an economic downturn; they've also come with a growing list of age-related health concerns, including type 2 diabetes, high blood pressure and heart disease. More than 75 million baby boomers are in the United States, and with such big numbers, the generation has always dictated huge shifts in societal norms. This time the shift they're creating is in health spending. The Centers for Medicare & Medicaid Services estimates that America's national health spending will reach $4.4 trillion a year by 2018—up from $2.5 trillion in 2009.[5]

As a notoriously well-informed category of consumers, baby boomers aren't just relying on traditional medicine to give them good health in their grandparenting years. They're also starting to customize their diets to promote good health. Indeed, 58 percent of baby boomers restrict at least one food in their diet (ranging from sodium to lactose) and 80 percent actively seek out foods made from whole grains.[6]

With baby boomers open to the possibilities of health through food, many doctors are now writing *food prescriptions* for their patients instead of drug prescriptions, taking advantage of the natural health properties that many whole foods—so-called "functional foods"—have. Here are just a few of the most well-known functional food recommendations baby boomers are eating up: almonds and oats to reduce the risk of coronary disease, omega-3 fatty acids–rich fish to lower cholesterol, tomatoes and broccoli to cut the risk of some types of cancer, and strawberries and kale to boost memory.

On the back of strong demand from baby boomers, the *Nutrition Business Journal* reported that consumers spent $39 billion on functional foods in 2010. Global Industry Analysts is predicting that by the time the youngest baby boomers pass 50—in 2015—the global market for functional foods will exceed $130 billion.[7] Capitalizing on this enormous and fast-growing market is simple: If you want baby boomers to buy your foods, allow them to customize the foods with the ingredients recommended by their doctors.

For more information about customizing your food for good health, including links to the innovative companies discussed in this chapter, visit CustomNation.com/Health.

Acknowledgments

Special thanks to Ava Bise, Kevin Flynn, Rodney Vencatachellum, Devi Vencatachellum, Marilyn Bise, Frances Albert, Lester Bise, Katie Newton, Norman E. Toy, Rebecca Voorwinde, Jaime Sneider, Kit Maloney, Barbara Rubin, David Sauvage, Frank Piller, Marc Cowlin, Dave Gross, Paul Blazek, Jessica Ritz, David Ritz, John Willig, Debbie Harmsen, Jennifer Canzeroni, Lindsay Marshall, Adrienne Lang, Lisa Miller, and Glenn Yeffeth.

About the Authors

Anthony Flynn. After graduating from the University of Southern California with a business degree in 2006, Flynn founded YouBar, the world's first customized nutrition bar company, with his mother, Ava Bise. Since then, Flynn has grown YouBar to seven-digit annual sales and employs 30 people in an 8,000-square-foot facility in downtown Los Angeles. Flynn frequently gives television, radio, newspaper and magazine interviews about YouBar and food customization. He has appeared on Fox, ABC, the Cooking Channel and NBC, among dozens of other television programs. He has also given interviews for *The New York Times, Women's Health,* Daily-Candy, the *Today* show, *E! News, The Nutrition Business Journal, Good Morning America,* and National Public Radio's *Marketplace.* In addition to this, Flynn gives lectures on how customization is changing the food industry, and he consults to companies launching customized food products. Among his numerous talks, he has been a guest speaker at USC, UC Berkeley and UCLA. When he isn't busy with YouBar and custom consulting (which is rare), Flynn can typically be found in his favorite gym (CrossFit Hollywood), going for a run up to the Hollywood sign or hanging out with friends.

Emily Flynn Vencat. After graduating from Barnard College, Columbia University with a degree in English Literature, Vencat moved to London in 2002, where she began her journalism career at *Newsweek.* Vencat worked as a London-based *Newsweek* correspondent for five years, where she covered major economic

189

trends, including the international housing market, the global luxury trade and the effects of global warming and the green movement on big business. After taking over as *Newsweek*'s London-based business writer in 2006, Vencat wrote more than 100 articles in two years, including five cover stories. Later, as a business writer on staff at The Associated Press, Vencat wrote blow-by-blow coverage of the 2008 global economic meltdown, with her articles being picked up by newspapers around the world, including the *International Herald Tribune* and *USA Today*. Vencat has interviewed some of the biggest names in the business world, including Virgin boss Richard Branson, Anglo American CEO Cynthia Carroll, Celtel founder Mo Ibrahim, Body Shop founder Anita Roddick and The Carlyle Group founding partner David Rubenstein. Vencat lives in Connecticut with her husband and two young sons.

Dennis Flynn (Lead Researcher). In 2007, at the age of 19, Flynn took over as YouBar's marketing, advertising and social media guru. Flynn's work helped catapult the company from a small five-person team the year he joined to a booming business with more than 30 employees just two years later. While running YouBar's marketing and advertising department, Flynn also completed his undergraduate degree in economics from the University of Southern California in 2010. Flynn currently lives in Los Angeles and is the director of marketing and social media at YouBar.

About YouBar

YouBar was launched in 2006 after the mother-and-son founders, Ava Bise and Anthony Flynn, began creating custom protein bars at home to meet their taste, health and allergy needs. They loved eating their unique bars so much that they thought there would be a huge market for customized protein bars made freshly to customers' own taste and nutritional needs. Anthony, who had just graduated from business school (and who has always had an irrepressible entrepreneurial spirit), said to his mom, "Let's launch a nutrition bar company," to which she replied, "Yes, if we can allow everyone to customize their bars like the ones we make at home."

And so in a small commercial kitchen in Los Angeles, YouBar was born. Since then YouBar has grown to 30 employees, has shipped as many as 10,000 custom bars in a day and has even been featured on a national television advertising campaign. The company has also worked closely with hundreds of dieticians, nutritionists, personal trainers, gyms, coffee shops and event planners to help them launch their own private-label energy bar product lines. YouBar now operates from an 8,000-square-foot facility in downtown Los Angeles. Its customized energy bars are based on the belief that no one else should decide what tastes good to us or what is good for our bodies.

Endnotes

Chapter One *The 21st Century's Custom Revolution*

1. Marc Cowlin, telephone interview by Anthony Flynn and Emily Flynn Vencat, May 2012. In 2011, CafePress' net revenue rose 37 percent to $176 million, and net income rose 33 percent to $3.6 million, compared to 2010.

Chapter Two *The End of Mass Production: How America Became a Custom Nation*

1. "You Choose," *The Economist*, December 16, 2010, www.economist .com/node/17723028. (Data in article from the Food Marketing Institute.)

2. Ibid.

3. Chris Anderson, *The Long Tail: Why the Future of Business Is Selling Less of More* (New York: Hyperion, 2008), 191.

4. www.youtube.com/watch?v=CJMsFGH4eoQ

5. The first Subway restaurant was opened in 1965 under the name "Pete's Super Submarines," but the restaurant did not become a franchise, or expand past the state of Connecticut until 1974. Information from Subway website, www.subway.com/subwayroot/about _us/history.aspx.

6. Pew Internet, "Internet Adoption Over Time," April 13, 2012. Report here—http://pewinternet.org/Reports/2012/Digital-differences/ Main-Report/Internet-adoption-over-time.aspx.

7. Estimates of typical retailer mark-ups come from Steven Greenhouse, "How Costco Became the Anti-Wal-Mart," *The New York Times*, July

17, 2005, www.nytimes.com/2005/07/17/business/yourmoney/17 costco.html?pagewanted=all.

8. Pew Internet, "Internet Adoption Over Time," April 13, 2012. Report here—http://pewinternet.org/Reports/2012/Digital-differences/Main-Report/Internet-adoption-over-time.aspx.

9. Treehouse Logic CEO Dave Sloan, interview by Anthony Flynn and Emily Flynn Vencat, October 14, 2011.

10. Boeing's Design Your Own 787 Dreamliner website: https://design yourown.newairplane.com.

11. Business Insider, "U.S. Smartphone Penetration Hits 50 Percent," by Alex Cocotas, March 30, 2012. http://articles.businessinsider.com /2012-03-30/news/31258792_1_smartphone-click-range.

12. Nathan Olivarez-Giles, "Average American spends equal time online and watching TV, report says" *Technology* (blog), *Los Angeles Times* December 13, 2010, http://latimesblogs.latimes.com/technology/2010 /12/average-american-spends-equal-time-surfing-the-web-and-watching -tv.html.

13. Kaiser Family Foundation study, "Generation M2: Media in the Lives of 8- to 18-Year-Olds," January 20, 2010, www.kff.org/entmedia /mh012010pkg.cfm.

14. At myL'Oreal.com, consumers can take detailed surveys to determine their own unique skin and hair types and receive "diagnostic" advice from top experts.

15. Our complete list of current customizing companies can be found in the appendix, and also on CustomNation.com.

16. "Private Equity and Venture Investors Offer Up $100M+ to Custom Clothing Firms," CB Insights (blog), www.cbinsights.com/blog/venture -capital/private-equity-and-venture-investors-offer-up-100m-to-custom -clothing-firms.

17. Erick Schonfeld, "Custom Clothier J. Hilburn Raises Another $5 Million and Adds Suits to Its Wardrobe," *Tech Crunch*, June 8, 2011, http://techcrunch.com/2011/06/08/j-hilburn-5-million-suits.

Chapter Three *Custom Generation: Why the 21st Century's Consumers*
                  Want Custom Everything

1. Jonathan Welsh, "What Does Generation Y Really Drive," *Driver's Seat* (blog), *The Wall Street Journal*, July 8, 2011. http://blogs.wsj.com /drivers-seat/2011/07/08/what-does-generation-y-really-drive. The data in *The Wall Street Journal* article comes from research done by TrueCar.com.

2. Pew Research. "The Millennials: Confident. Connected. Open to Change," February 24, 2010.

3. M. J. Stephy, "Gen-X: The Ignored Generation?" *Time*, April 16, 2008, www.time.com/time/arts/article/0,8599,1731528,00.html. There are roughly 46 million members of Generation X, according to *Time*, which defines Gen X as those born between 1965 and 1980.

4. Figure comes from www.gen-we.com home page.

5. *The New York Times*, "E-Tailor Customization: Convenient or Creepy?" by Natasha Singer, June 23, 2012. www.nytimes.com/2012/06/24/ technology/e-tailer-customization-whats-convenient-and-whats-just -plain-creepy.html?_r=1&ref=todayspaper&nl=business&emc=dlbka 34_20120625.

6. Jean M. Twenge, *Generation Me: Why Today's Young Americans Are More Confident, Assertive, Entitled—and More Miserable Than Ever Before* (New York City: Free Press, 2006).

7. Carmen Magar, phone interview with Anthony Flynn and Emily Flynn Vencat, company sales data from October 2010.

8. Cathy Benko, "Mass Career Customization: From Corporate Ladder to Corporate Lattice" (lecture, World Conference on Mass Customization, Personalization and Co-Creation, San Francisco, CA, November 16, 2011).

9. Pew Research Center study, "Millennials: A Portrait of Generation Next," February 2010, 51, http://pewresearch.org/pubs/1501 /millennials-new-survey-generational-personality-upbeat-open-new -ideas-technology-bound.

10. Robert P. Jones, Daniel Cox and Elizabeth Cook, "Generations at Odds: The Millennial Generation and the Future of Gay and Lesbian Rights," Public Religion Research Institute, August 2011, http://public religion.org/research/2011/08/generations-at-odds.

11. Benko lecture, November 2011.

Chapter Four *The Paradox of Choice*

1. www.ford.com/cars/mustang/customizer/?intcmp=fv-experience -hero-ford-mustang. Accessed January 2012.

2. The New York Times Book Review, "Indecision Making," by Virginia Postrel, April 15, 2010.

3. Dan Ariely, *The Honest Truth About Dishonesty: How We Lie to Everyone— Especially Ourselves* (HarperCollins: New York, 2012). Dan's book is a riveting study of morality, which I highly recommend.

4. Michael I. Norton, Daniel Mochon and Dan Ariely, "The 'IKEA Effect': When Labor Leads to Love," *Journal of Consumer Psychology* (2011).

5. Ibid., pg. 3.

6. Nikolaus Franke, Martin Schreier and Ulrike Kaiser, "The 'I Designed It Myself' Effect in Mass Customization," *Management Science*, 56 (1), 125–40.

7. Data for this chart comes from two research papers: The "IKEA Effect" (Ikea boxes and origami) and "The 'I Designed It Myself' Effect in Mass Customization" (skis and T-shirts).

8. Kyle Alspach, "Gemvara raises $25M in quest to become world's largest jeweler," *Boston Business Journal*, June 4, 2012.

Chapter Five *Made in the YOU.S.A.: Why Customizers Manufacture in America (Or Wherever Their Customers Are)*

1. http://blog.zazzle.com/2010/10/22/meg-whitman-and-nyc-mayor -michael-bloomberg-tour-zazzle.

2. "Moving Back to America," *The Economist*, May 12, 2011, www .economist.com/node/18682182.

3. The Boston Consulting Group, "More Than a Third of Large Manufacturers Are Considering Reshoring from China to the U.S," news release, April 20, 2012, www.bcg.com/media/PressReleaseDetails .aspx?id=tcm:12-104216.

4. Ibid.

5. Stefany Moore, "Germany's Spreadshirt.com grows its U.S. business with a customization platform," *InternetRetailer.com*, October 27, 2011, www.internetretailer.com/2011/10/27/spreadshirtcom-grows-its-us -business-customization.

6. In my following discussion of this battle, I'll be discussing the core differences between the single largest companies in Gap Inc. and Inditex Group's holdings. Gap Inc. owns a collection of other clothing companies, including Old Navy and Banana Republic. Likewise, in addition to Zara, Inditex also owns clothing companies like Bershka and Pull & Bear. However, Gap Inc.'s largest company is Gap and Inditex's largest is Zara. And so, in the following discussion, I'll be using these two core brands to illustrate the difference between the two clothing behemoths.

7. John M. Gallaugher, "Zara Case: Fast Fashion from Savvy Systems," in *Information Systems: A Manager's Guide to Harnessing Technology* (Irvington, New York: Flat World Knowledge Inc., 2010), 2. (Page numbers are from the version of the chapter that was published alone, in 2008, before book publication.)

8. The first Zara store opened in the small Spanish city of A Coruña in 1975, but the company's huge global expansion didn't begin until parent company Inditex Group offered its first IPO in 2001. The IPO, which was 26 times oversubscribed, raised 2.1 billion euros in exchange for 23 percent of the firm. Richard Heller, "Inside Zara," *Forbes.com*, May 28, 2001, www.forbes.com/global/2001/0528/024 .html.

9. John M. Gallaugher, "Zara Case: Fast Fashion from Savvy Systems."

10. Patricia Sellers, "Gap's New Guy Upstairs," *Fortune*, April 14, 2003, http://money.cnn.com/magazines/fortune/fortune_archive/2003/04/14/340905/index.htm.

Chapter Six *The Future of Commerce: Customize Everything, Everywhere, All the Time*

1. It is worth noting that all these companies get their designs from a diverse community of users, which includes professional and amateur designers. You could go to any of these sites and design your own object for 3-D printing today.

2. 2011 Author interview with Jeff Lipton, the head of Cornell's Fab@ Home program.

3. Netflix considers its recommendation service so vital that, in 2009, it awarded $1 million to a team that improved its accuracy.

4. "Waste Land: Does the Large Amount of Food Discarded in the U.S. Take a Toll on the Environment?" *Scientific American*, March 3, 2010, www.scientificamerican.com/article.cfm?id=earth-talk-waste-land.

5. *The Washington Post*, "Hunger a Growing Problem in America, USDA reports," by Amy Goldstein, April 17, 2009. www.washingtonpost.com/wp-dyn/content/article/2009/11/16/AR2009111601598.html.

Chapter Seven *Launching Your New CIY Business*

1. This quote comes from an interview that Anita Roddick gave Dennis Hughes and Janice Hughes of Share Guide Publishers. The published interview is undated, but can be found here: www.shareguide.com/Roddick.html.

2. The Kauffman Foundation, "Jobless Entrepreneurship Tarnishes Steady Rate of US Start-Up Activity, Kauffman Study Shows," news release, March 7, 2011, www.kauffman.org/newsroom/jobless-entrepreneurship-tarnishes-steady-rate-of-us-startup-activity.aspx (This paper includes data showing that Americans created 565,000 new businesses in 2010 alone).

3. *Entrepreneur*, "10 Hot Startup Sectors for New Business Ideas in 2012," November 29, 2011. Customization is "Trend Number 3." www .entrepreneur.com/slideshow/220748.

4. This team includes cyLEDGE Media GmbH, IndiValue Softwareentwicklungs GmbH and eworx Network & Internet GmbH.

5. Author interview with Paul Blazek, the head of cyLEDGE, in November 2011.

6. *Business Insider*. This data comes from 2010, when Google made revenues of $29 billion in online advertising.

Chapter Eight *Adding CIY to Your Existing Business*

1. Prices referenced here and in the accompanying chart are the prices from January 2012.

2. "Is Santa a Deadweight Loss?" *The Economist*, December 20, 2001, www.economist.com/node/885748?story_id=885748.

3. Gary Rivlin, "When Buying a Diamond Starts With a Mouse," *The New York Times*, January 7, 2007, www.nytimes.com/2007/01/07 /business/yourmoney/07nile.html?pagewanted=all.

4. Rupal Parekh, "Personalized Products Please, But Can They Create Profit?" *Advertising Age*, May 21, 2012, http://adage.com/article /news/personalized-products-create-profit/234838/.

5. PepsiCo, "Walkers 'Do Us A Flavour,'" news release, October 21, 2008, www.pepsico.co.uk/our-company/trade-information/trade-media -centre/trade-news/walkers-do-us-a-flavour.

6. Ibid.

7. Manning Gottlieb, "Walkers 'Do Us a Flavour' case study," *UTalkMarketing.com*, July 19, 2010, www.utalkmarketing.com/Pages/Article .aspx?ArticleID=18384.

8. "Mountain Dew Voltage Wins DEWmocracy Vote," *Bev Review*, August 19, 2008, www.bevreview.com/2008/08/19/news-mountain -dew-voltage-wins-dewmocracy-vote.

Chapter Nine *The Seven Crucial Lessons of Customizing*

1. Bloomberg, "Kodak Worth More in Breakup with $3 Billion Patents: Real M&A," August 17, 2011. www.bloomberg.com/news/2011-08 -17/kodak-worth-five-times-more-in-breakup-with-3-billion-patents -real-m-a.html.

2. Small Business Advice TV interview on December 4, 2008. The interview can be viewed online at http://talktalk.studiotalk.tv/chat /michael_dell_exclusive_interview.

3. *Business Insider*, "The Digital 100: The World's Most Valuable Start-ups," September 23, 2010. www.businessinsider.com/digital-100? op=1

Chapter Ten *Customize Your Marketing*

1. Nielsen, "State of the Media: The Social Media Report," Q3 2011, http://blog.nielsen.com/nielsenwire/social/.

2. Chris Barry, Rob Markey, Eric Almquist and Chris Brahm, "Putting Social Media to Work," Bain & Company, September 12, 2011. www.bain.com/publications/articles/putting-social-media-to-work .aspx.

3. Paul Marsden, "Social Commerce Makeover: 7 Things Your Brand Should Be Doing Today—Summary & Link to Fluid Webinar," *Social Commerce Today*, June 4, 2010, http://socialcommercetoday.com/social -commerce-makeover-7-things-your-brand-should-be-doing-today -summary-link-to-fluid-webinar.

4. *Entrepreneur*, "10 Hot Startup Sectors for New Business Ideas in 2012," November 29, 2011. http://www.entrepreneur.com/slide show/220748#.

5. Forbes.com, "Need To Build A Community? Learn From Thread-less," by Laurie Burkitt, January 7, 2010. www.forbes.com/2010 /01/06/threadless-t-shirt-community-crowdsourcing-cmo-network -threadless.html.

6. Jennifer Van Grove, "Dunkin Donuts Wants You To Create Its Next Donut," *Mashable Social Media*, February 8, 2010, http://mashable

.com/2010/02/08/dunkin-donuts-contest. It is interesting to note that, while customers have created more than 1 million doughnuts on Dunkin' Donuts "Create" website, only 220,000 were submitted to the competition. Indeed, in the first year alone (2009) a full 269,000 doughnuts were created after the competition was over, according to Mashable, showing that consumers are having fun creating doughnuts online and not just doing it to win.

7. Ann Handley, "The Importance of Sharing: Everything You Need to Know about Generating Leads You Learned in Kindergarten." *Entrepreneur*, December 12, 2011, www.entrepreneur.com/article /220720.

8. Nathan Olivarez-Giles, "Facebook F8: Redesigning and Hitting 800 Million Users," *Technology* (blog), *Los Angeles Times*, September 22, 2011, http://latimesblogs.latimes.com/technology/2011/09/facebook -f8-media-features.html.

9. Nielsen, "State of the Media" report, Q3 2011.

10. Ibid.

Chapter Eleven *Keep Growing Your CIY Business*

1. Dominik Walcher and Frank Piller. *The Customization 500: An International Benchmark Study on Mass Customization and Personalization in Consumer E-Commerce*, November 17, 2011.

Afterword

1. Kannayiram Alagiakrishnan and Anitha Chopra, "Health and Health Care of Asian Indian American Elders," www.Stanford.edu/group /ethnoger/asianindian.html.

2. Interleukin Genetics Inc., "Interleukin Genetics, Inc. and Stanford University Report Genetic Test Improves Weight Loss Success With Diets," news release, March 3, 2010 www.prnewswire.com /news-releases/interleukin-genetics-inc-and-stanford-university -report-genetic-test-improves-weight-loss-success-with-diets-86252 902.html.

3. Jerome Groopman, "The Peanut Puzzle," *The New Yorker*, February 2011, www.newyorker.com/reporting/2011/02/07/110207fa_fact_groopman.

4. Global Industry Analysts, "Food Allergy and Intolerance Products: A Global Strategic Business Report," April 1, 2011, www.companiesand markets.com/Market-Report/food-allergy-and-intolerance-products -a-global-strategic-business-report-618319.asp?prk=7c4ed5b510c1ffe 12b50d9829eddaba2.

5. Jessica Rao, "Bust of the Baby Boomer Economy: 'Generation Spend' Tightens Belt," CNBC, January 21, 2010, www.cnbc.com/id /34941331/Bust_of_the_Baby_Boomer_Economy_Generation_ Spend_Tightens_Belt and *Improving Health Care Cost Projections for the Medicare Population Summary of a Workshop National Research Council (US) Committee on National Statistics* (Washington: National Academies Press, 2010), www.ncbi.nlm.nih.gov/books/NBK52814.

6. "Most Americans Are Health-Conscious, But Behavior Varies By Age," Harris Interactive poll, April 27, 2011, www.harrisinteractive .com/NewsRoom/HarrisPolls/tabid/447/mid/1508/articleId/762 /ctl/ReadCustom%20Default/Default.aspx.

7. Alissa Marrapodi, "Postmodern Nutrition: Functional Foods, Beverages," *Natural Products Insider*, September 22, 2011, www.natural productsinsider.com/articles/2011/09/postmodern-nutrition -functional-foods-beverages.aspx.

Appendix: Chart of the World's Customizing Companies

	Company	Order Online?	Product	Industries	Country
1	1154 LILL	Yes	Bag	Accessories	US
2	121 TIME	Yes	Watch	Accessories	CH
3	123 Skins	Yes	Skins	Electronics	DE
4	3D supply	Yes	T-Shirt	Apparel	DE
5	4foto	Yes	Photo Canvas	Print	DE
6	Aberdeen	Yes	Computer	Electronics	US
7	adagio teas	Yes	Tea	Food	US
8	Adam Opel	No	Car	Automobile	DE
9	Adiamor	Yes	Jewelry	Accessories	US
10	Adidas	Yes	Shoes	Footwear	US
11	Advantage Bridal	Yes	Shirt	Apparel	US
12	Advent Man	Yes	Christmas Calendar	Giftware	DE
13	AEZ Leichtmetallräder	No	Car Wheel	Automobile	DE
14	Agando	Yes	Computer	Electronics	DE
15	Akkukonfigurator	Yes	Rechargeable Battery	Electronics	DE
16	AktionsLicht	Yes	Lantern	Giftware	DE
17	Alco	No	Winter Garden	Construction	AT
18	Aletoware	Yes	Computer	Electronics	DE
19	Alfa Romeo	No	Car	Automobile	DE
20	allmyTea	Yes	Tea	Food	DE
21	Alphabet Plates	Yes	Meal Goods	Children's Products	US
22	Alternate	Yes	PC	Electronics	DE
23	Alulux	No	Roller Blind	House & Garden	DE
24	aluni	Yes	T-Shirt	Apparel	AT
25	American Golf	Yes	Golf Ball	Sport & Leisure	US
26	Amodoro	No	Jewelry	Accessories	DE
27	Amoonic	Yes	Jewelry	Accessories	DE
28	animaxx	Yes	Flip-Book	Giftware	DE
29	animaxx	Yes	Thumb Cinema	Entertainment	DE
30	Antero	Yes	Snowboard	Sport & Leisure	AT
31	apfelshop	Yes	Computer	Electronics	AT
32	ARMADA	No	Clothes	Apparel	US
33	artido	Yes	Photo Products	Print	DE
34	Artistic Checks	Yes	Giftware	Giftware	US
35	ArtYourFace	Yes	Pop-Art Photo	Giftware	DE
36	ATB	No	Engines	Automobile	AT

	Company	Order Online?	Product	Industries	Country
37	ATELCO	Yes	Computer	Electronics	DE
38	Atelier Goldner Schnitt	Yes	Clothes	Apparel	AT
39	Audena	Yes	Furniture	Furniture	DE
40	Audi Deutschland	No	Car	Automobile	DE
41	Austad's Golf	Yes	Golf Equipment	Sport & Leisure	US
42	aYoh	No	Merchandise Products	Advertising Material	DE
43	baby-strampler.ch	Yes	Baby Equipment	Children's Products	CH
44	Bags-Purses-Totes	Yes	Bag	Accessories	US
45	Baked By Melissa	No	Cupcake	Food	US
46	Bamford Watch Department	Yes	Watch	Accessories	US
47	Banana Moon	Yes	Clothes	Apparel	US
48	Barrels & Bottles	Yes	Wine Label	Print	UK
49	BAUER	No	Irrigation System	House & Garden	AT
50	Baur Versand	Yes	Shirt	Apparel	DE
51	Bayerwald	No	Window	Construction	DE
52	beaniebee	Yes	T-Shirt	Apparel	DE
53	beau-coup	Yes	Giftware	Giftware	US
54	Beer Stickr	Yes	Beer Label	Giftware	DE
55	BEICK	Yes	Bicycle	Sport & Leisure	NL
56	berlinbag	Yes	Bag	Accessories	DE
57	Best 4 Balls	Yes	Golf Ball	Sport & Leisure	UK
58	BestCustomShirt.com	Yes	T-Shirt	Apparel	US
59	Betonwerk Rieder	No	Noise Barrier	Construction	AT
60	BEYOND	Yes	Jacket	Apparel	US
61	Bicycle-Love	Yes	Bicycle	Sport & Leisure	DE
62	Bieberer Brillenladen	Yes	Sport Sunglasses	Optician	DE
63	BIG HUGE LABS	No	Wallpaper	Print	US
64	Bike by Me	Yes	Bicycle	Sport & Leisure	SE
65	Bike Direkt	No	Bicycle	Sport & Leisure	AT
66	Bio Fit	No	Chair	Furniture	US
67	Biogolftee.com	Yes	Golf Equipment	Sport & Leisure	AT
68	Bivolino.com	Yes	Shirt	Apparel	BE
69	Blancier BV	Yes	Watch	Accessories	US
70	Blank Label Group	Yes	Shirt	Apparel	US
71	blazingclothing	Yes	T-Shirt	Apparel	UK
72	Blends For Friends	Yes	Tea	Giftware	US

	Company	Order Online?	Product	Industries	Country
73	BlockAmps.com	Yes	Amplifier	Music	US
74	BlueCotton	Yes	T-Shirt	Apparel	US
75	Bluenile	Yes	Ring	Accessories	UK
76	Blurb	No	Book	Print	US
77	BMW	No	Car	Automobile	DE
78	BMW Mini	No	Car	Automobile	DE
79	Boarddesigner	Yes	Snowboard	Sport & Leisure	AT
80	BOARDPUSHER	Yes	Skateboard	Sport & Leisure	US
81	Bob Books	Yes	Flickbook	Print	UK
82	Böckmann	No	Car & Horse Trailer	Automobile	DE
83	Brand Devil	Yes	Electronics	Electronics	DE
84	brandmybook	Yes	Book	Print	DE
85	Brewtopia	Yes	Label For Bottle	Giftware	US
86	Brillant-Aquarium	Yes	Aquarium	Equipment For Pets	DE
87	Brown Eyed Baby Boutique	Yes	Baby Equipment	Children's Products	US
88	Brügmann Traum Garten	No	Playground	Construction	DE
89	Brunswick Bowling & Billiards Corporation	Yes	Pool Table	Sport & Leisure	US
90	Buchbinderei Obermeier	No	Notebook	Stationery	DE
91	BUGATTI	No	Car	Automobile	FR
92	Build-A-Bear Workshop	Yes	Teddy Bear	Children's Products	US
93	BULBBY	Yes	Giftware	Children's Products	NL
94	Buy-Tees.com	Yes	T-Shirt	Apparel	US
95	CafePress.com	Yes	T-Shirt	Apparel	US
96	Came & Leon	Yes	Bag	Accessories	DE
97	CAMPE & OHFF	Yes	Shirt	Apparel	DE
98	Candybarwrapper	Yes	Candy Bar Wrapper	Print	US
99	Cardboards	Yes	Kiteboard	Sport & Leisure	AU
100	Carnac	No	Shoes	Footwear	IT
101	Cays	Yes	Bag	Accessories	DE
102	ccw-online	Yes	Computer	Electronics	DE
103	CharGrilled	Yes	T-Shirt	Apparel	UK
104	Chevrolet Deutschland	No	Car	Automobile	DE
105	chiligreen	Yes	Computer	Electronics	AT
106	Choccreate	Yes	Chocolate	Food	US
107	Chocolate Style	Yes	Chocolate	Food	DE

	Company	Order Online?	Product	Industries	Country
108	Chocolato.de	Yes	Chocolate	Food	DE
109	Chocomize	Yes	Chocolate	Food	US
110	chocri	Yes	Chocolate	Food	DE
111	ChoiceShirts	Yes	T-Shirt	Apparel	US
112	Citroen	No	Car	Automobile	UK
113	Clopay	No	Garage Door	Construction	US
114	Clothes2Order.com	Yes	T-Shirt	Apparel	UK
115	Customized Mortgage Solutions	No	Mortgage	Service	US
116	CocoaBella Chocolates	Yes	Chocolate Box	Food	US
117	Coco Myles	Yes	Bridesmaid Dress	Apparel	US
118	codeME	Yes	T-Shirt	Apparel	DE
119	ColorWare	Yes	Electronics	Electronics	US
120	COLOURlovers	No	Pattern	Media	US
121	Columbus	Yes	Laptop Sleeve	Accessories	DE
122	Comboutique.com	Yes	T-Shirt	Apparel	FR
123	CONE DRIVE	No	Cone Drive	Steel	US
124	Connect	No	Door	Construction	UK
125	Conrad Electronic	Yes	Computer	Electronics	AT
126	Contento	Yes	Giftware	Giftware	DE
127	Continental	No	Car Wheel	Automobile	DE
128	Converse	Yes	Shoes	Footwear	US
129	cookiemania	Yes	Cookie	Food	DE
130	Corporate Casuals	No	Clothes	Apparel	US
131	CowCrowd	No	Lifestyle Accessory	Accessories	AT
132	Crayola	Yes	Pen	Stationery	US
133	Created 4 Me	Yes	Children's Book	Print	US
134	cupboardyourway	Yes	Cupboard	Furniture	DE
135	CurlyQ Cuties	Yes	Plush Monster	Children's Products	US
136	Custom Camera Collection	Yes	Camera	Electronics	US
137	Custom GelPaxs Inc.	Yes	Gel Pack	Giftware	US
138	CustomGlamGirl.com	Yes	T-Shirt	Apparel	US
139	Customink	Yes	T-Shirt	Apparel	US
140	Customized Classics	Yes	Book	Print	US
141	CustomizedGirl	Yes	T-Shirt	Apparel	US
142	CustomizedGolfBalls.com	Yes	Golf Ball	Sport & Leisure	US
143	customizedswimsuit.com	Yes	Swim Suit	Sport & Leisure	US

	Company	Order Online?	Product	Industries	Country
144	Customized World	Yes	T-Shirt	Apparel	US
145	Custom Made For Kids	Yes	Book	Print	US
146	Custom Marine Carpet	Yes	Floor Mat	House & Garden	US
147	Custom Storybooks	Yes	Children's Book	Print	US
148	Custom Wine Source	Yes	Wine Label	Print	US
149	Daihatsu Deutschland	No	Car	Automobile	DE
150	Daimler AG	No	Car	Automobile	DE
151	damao	Yes	Furniture	Furniture	DE
152	dammitmanstuff.com	Yes	T-Shirt	Apparel	US
153	Dann Clothing	Yes	Shirt	Apparel	US
154	DeinBonbon	Yes	Candy	Food	DE
155	deineTorte.de	Yes	Cake	Food	DE
156	deinSekt.de	Yes	Sparkling Wine Label	Giftware	DE
157	DELL	Yes	Computer	Electronics	US
158	Delusha	Yes	Jewelry	Accessories	ES
159	Der Fahrradladen	No	Bicycle	Sport & Leisure	DE
160	Design a cake	Yes	Cake	Food	AU
161	designashirt	Yes	T-Shirt	Apparel	US
162	Design a Tea	Yes	Tea	Food	US
163	Designathong.com	Yes	Underwear	Apparel	US
164	Design-her Gals	No	Giftware	Giftware	US
165	Design Skins	Yes	Skins	Electronics	DE
166	Design your own card	Yes	Office Equipment	Stationery	US
167	DesignYourWeddingRings.com	Yes	Ring	Accessories	US
168	Deutsche Post.com	Yes	Card	Print	DE
169	Deutsche Post.de	Yes	Newspaper	Print	DE
170	Diamond Heaven	Yes	Jewelry	Accessories	UK
171	Diamonds.com	Yes	Jewelry	Accessories	US
172	Dietrich Maßhemden	No	Shirt	Apparel	DE
173	DIFFERENCES	No	Ski	Sport & Leisure	AT
174	DigiLabs	Yes	Greeting Card	Stationery	US
175	DiTech	Yes	Computer	Electronics	AT
176	Diva Entertains	Yes	Soap	Beauty	US
177	Divine Digitizing	Yes	T-Shirt	Apparel	US
178	Dolzer Online Shop	Yes	Shirt	Apparel	DE
179	DOMYJEANS	Yes	Jeans	Apparel	US

	Company	Order Online?	Product	Industries	Country
180	Doogma Tec	No	Embed Configurators	Service	US
181	Drei Gürteltiere	Yes	Belt	Accessories	DE
182	DressByDesign	Yes	Clothes	Apparel	US
183	Drumwerx	Yes	Drum Set	Music	US
184	Dunlop	No	Car Wheel	Automobile	DE
185	Easytissue	Yes	Tissue Box	Giftware	NL
186	eCreamery	Yes	Ice Cream	Food	US
187	ED HOME	Yes	Mat	Furniture	AT
188	eFavorMart.com	Yes	Giftware	Giftware	US
189	einkaufstrolley.de	Yes	Trolley	House & Garden	DE
190	EINS-WIE-KEINS	Yes	Book	Print	DE
191	elemental THREADS	Yes	Bag	Accessories	US
192	element bars	Yes	Nutrition Bar	Food	US
193	e.l.f.	Yes	Make-Up	Beauty	DE
194	Eli's Cheesecake	Yes	Cake	Food	US
195	engelbert strauss	No	Business Clothes	Apparel	AT
196	ENOUGH MERCH	Yes	T-Shirt	Apparel	DE
197	Esens Fragrances	Yes	Perfume	Beauty	US
198	Eshirt	Yes	T-Shirt	Apparel	IT
199	e-Shirt.com	Yes	T-Shirt	Apparel	US
200	E-Skylight	Yes	Skylight	Steel	US
201	e-tec	Yes	Computer	Electronics	AT
202	eterna	Yes	Shirt	Apparel	DE
203	Evlove Intimates	Yes	Lingerie	Apparel	US
204	Expertshirt	Yes	T-Shirt	Apparel	US
205	Extra Film	Yes	Print	Giftware	BE
206	Eyewearcases.com	Yes	Glasses Case	Optician	US
207	fabidoo	Yes	USB Stick	Giftware	DE
208	Fabric on Demand	Yes	Fabrics	Apparel	US
209	fakemagazines.com	Yes	Magazine Covers	Print	US
210	Fanmarkt.de	Yes	T-Shirt	Apparel	DE
211	Feather River Doors	No	Door	Construction	US
212	Fensternorm	No	Window	Construction	AT
213	Ferrari.com	No	Car	Automobile	IT
214	FIAT	No	Car	Automobile	DE
215	Fiat / Lancia	No	Car	Automobile	DE
216	fill in the blankie	Yes	Baby Blanket	Children's Products	US

	Company	Order Online?	Product	Industries	Country
217	Filzed	Yes	Handy Bag	Accessories	DE
218	Finestly	Yes	Bag	Accessories	DE
219	Flirt Shirts	Yes	T-Shirt	Apparel	AT
220	flockstoff.com	Yes	T-Shirt	Apparel	DE
221	Fluid Forms	Yes	Streets Clock	Giftware	AT
222	Foghorn	Yes	T-Shirt	Apparel	AU
223	Food Box	Yes	Cook Book	Print	DE
224	Footjoy	Yes	Shoes	Footwear	US
226	Ford Motor Company	No	Car	Automobile	US
227	FotoBed.com	Yes	Bedding	House & Garden	US
228	fotokasten	Yes	Photo Book	Print	DE
229	fotopost24	No	Photo Products	Giftware	DE
230	fotopuzzle.de	Yes	Photo Puzzle	Giftware	DE
231	Franklin+Gower	Yes	Clothes	Apparel	US
232	freddy & ma	Yes	Handbag	Accessories	US
233	FREITAG	Yes	Bag	Accessories	CH
234	FunnyUndies.com	Yes	Underwear	Apparel	US
235	GemKitty Jewelry	Yes	Jewelry	Accessories	US
236	Genometri	Yes	Picture Frame	Giftware	US
237	Ghost Nest	Yes	Door Knob	Furniture	US
238	Gilletts Jewellers	No	Ring	Accessories	AU
239	Gloria J Designs	Yes	Wine Label	Print	US
240	Glücksgeschenk	Yes	Horse Shoe	Giftware	NL
241	Golfballs.com	Yes	Golf Ball	Sport & Leisure	US
242	Golfsmith	Yes	Golf Equipment	Sport & Leisure	US
243	golfteesplus	Yes	Golf Tees	Sport & Leisure	US
244	Grateful Body	Yes	Body Products	Beauty	US
245	Great Create	Yes	Dog Tag	Accessories	LT
246	GreekGear	Yes	T-Shirt	Apparel	US
247	Gresso	No	Mobile Phone Cover	Giftware	US
248	gumdrop cookie shop	Yes	Cookie	Print	US
249	haircare4me	No	Shampoo	Beauty	DE
250	Hand Picked Pumpkin	Yes	Clothes	Children's Products	US
251	Handy-Aufkleber.de	Yes	Cell Phone Sticker	Giftware	DE
252	Handysocken.ch	Yes	Mobile Phone Cover	Giftware	CH
253	Hanse	No	Yacht	Transportation	DE

	Company	Order Online?	Product	Industries	Country
254	Harley Davidson.com	No	Motorcycle	Automobile	US
255	Harmony Designs	Yes	Bookmark	Stationery	US
256	HatTail Headwear	Yes	Hat	Accessories	US
257	HC	Yes	License Plate	Automobile	DE
258	Heineken	Yes	Bottle Design	Print	NL
259	Heizstrahlershop	No	Radiant Heater	Electronics	DE
260	Hella	No	Electronics	Electronics	DE
261	hemdschneider	Yes	Shirt	Apparel	DE
262	hemdwerk UG	Yes	Shirt	Apparel	DE
263	Hera	No	Luminaire	Construction	DE
264	Hershey's Store	Yes	Chocolate	Food	US
265	HEULTEC	Yes	Signal Circular Connector	Electronics	DE
266	Hit-Bikes Bikestore	No	Bicycle	Sport & Leisure	DE
267	Holl	Yes	Shirt	Apparel	IT
268	Homesafe	Yes	Door	Construction	UK
269	HONDA	No	Car	Automobile	DE
270	Horsefeathers store	No	Clothes	Apparel	CZ
271	HYMER	No	Camper	Transportation	DE
272	HYUNDAI	No	Car	Automobile	DE
273	Ibex	No	Bicycle	Sport & Leisure	CH
274	IC3D	Yes	Pants	Apparel	US
275	idbeer	Yes	Label For Bottle	Print	DE
276	ideck	Yes	Deck Design	Sport & Leisure	DE
277	iloux	No	Electronics	Electronics	DE
278	ILoveTShirts.net	Yes	T-Shirt	Apparel	US
279	i.materialise	Yes	3D Model	Construction	US
280	Indishirt MAASSWERK	Yes	T-Shirt	Apparel	DE
281	Indochino	Yes	Suit	Apparel	US
282	Initial Impressions	Yes	Baby Equipment	Children's Products	US
283	INKtastic	Yes	Giftware	Giftware	US
284	Inmod.com	Yes	Bed Linen	House & Garden	US
285	In The Paper.com	Yes	Newspaper	Print	UK
286	'In Toon'	Yes	Comic Book Cover	Print	US
287	Inwerk	Yes	Furniture	Furniture	DE

	Company	Order Online?	Product	Industries	Country
288	iPrint.com	Yes	Office Equipment	Stationery	US
289	I See Me!	Yes	Book	Print	US
290	Islandwolle Versand	No	Pullover	Apparel	DE
291	iTailor.com	Yes	Shirt	Apparel	DE
292	Jagsch Tischlerei	No	Floor Mat	House & Garden	DE
293	Jaguar	No	Car	Automobile	US
294	JamesAllen.com	Yes	Jewelry	Accessories	US
295	Jan Ulrich Bikes	Yes	Bicycle	Sport & Leisure	DE
296	JasonL	Yes	Office Equipment	Furniture	AU
297	JazzyShirt	Yes	T-Shirt	Apparel	DE
298	Jellyfish.com	Yes	Swim Suit	Sport & Leisure	AU
299	Jely Haus	No	House	Construction	DE
300	JL Hufford	Yes	Coffee	Food	US
301	John Deere	No	Agricultural Tractor	Transportation	DE
302	Jolly Books	Yes	Book	Giftware	DE
303	Jonathan Adler	Yes	Furniture	Furniture	US
304	Juicy Walls	Yes	Wall Hangings	House & Garden	DE
305	JULIE & GRACE	Yes	Jewelry	Accessories	DE
306	Just Jen	Yes	Shirt	Apparel	US
307	Kantenbänder	Yes	Table Tennis	Sport & Leisure	DE
308	Karibu	No	Sauna	House & Garden	DE
309	Karl Baisch	Yes	Dentist Furniture	Furniture	DE
310	Keds	Yes	Shoes	Footwear	US
311	Keller&Kalmbach	No	Storage System	Construction	DE
312	Kenngott Treppen	No	Stairs	Construction	DE
313	KERN-Energie	Yes	Cereal	Food	DE
314	Kern-Haus	No	Prefabricated House	Construction	DE
315	Kitchen Studio	No	Kitchen	House & Garden	NZ
316	Kleenex	No	Tissue Label	Giftware	US
317	kleidershop24.ch	Yes	T-Shirt	Apparel	CH
318	K&M Computer	Yes	Computer	Electronics	DE
319	Koba	No	Bicycle	Sport & Leisure	CH
320	Koga-Signature	No	Bicycle	Sport & Leisure	NL
321	koordinatenshirt.com	Yes	T-Shirt	Apparel	CH
322	Kraftstoff Bike	No	Bicycle	Sport & Leisure	AT
323	Krassolade	Yes	Chocolate	Food	DE

	Company	Order Online?	Product	Industries	Country
324	Krines	No	Window	Construction	DE
325	K-Swiss	Yes	Shoes	Footwear	US
326	Kuchen-im-Glas	Yes	Cake	Food	DE
327	Kuchenkurier	Yes	Cake	Food	DE
328	Labello	No	Lip Gloss	Beauty	DE
329	lage000.at	Yes	T-Shirt	Apparel	AT
330	LAMPS PLUS	Yes	Lamp	Furniture	US
331	LaserPartner	Yes	Laser-Crystal	Giftware	DE
332	Latschen	Yes	Flip Flops	Footwear	DE
333	Laudi Vidni	Yes	Handbag	Accessories	US
334	Legamaster	No	Board	Construction	DE
335	Lexus	No	Car	Automobile	US
336	Lids	Yes	Baseball Cap	Accessories	US
337	LikeMyCase	Yes	Mobile Phone Cover	Giftware	UK
338	Lilie Customized Cosmetics	Yes	Lipstick	Beauty	US
339	Limberry	Yes	Clothes	Apparel	DE
340	Limoges Jewelry	Yes	Jewelry	Accessories	US
341	Linde	No	Gases	Chemistry	DE
342	Lind Golf	Yes	Golf Club	Sport & Leisure	AU
343	Liste Rouge Imagine	Yes	Shirt	Apparel	US
344	Liste Rouge Paris	Yes	Shirt	Apparel	US
345	Loewe.	No	Television	Electronics	DE
346	logiprint.com	Yes	T-Shirt	Apparel	DE
347	Logo Print	Yes	Golf Ball	Sport & Leisure	US
348	LogoSportswear	Yes	Sports Wear	Apparel	US
349	Longcamp	Yes	Bag	Accessories	FR
350	Louis Vuitton	Yes	Bag	Accessories	US
351	LoveLee Studio	Yes	Handbag	Accessories	US
352	lovelylabels	Yes	Business Card	Stationery	US
353	LTL Prints	Yes	Wallpaper	Print	US
354	Lucrin	Yes	Leather Products	Accessories	CH
355	Lulette	Yes	Scarf	Apparel	US/CA
356	LunaArt	Yes	T-Shirt	Apparel	DE
357	Made to Measure Blinds UK	Yes	Blinds	Construction	UK
358	MAHRENHOLZ	No	Door	Construction	DE
359	Make Your Own Jeans	Yes	Clothes	Apparel	IN
360	MAM	Yes	Pacifier	Children's Products	AT

	Company	Order Online?	Product	Industries	Country
361	Manning&Manning	Yes	Shirt	Apparel	UK
362	Manroof	Yes	T-Shirt	Apparel	CH
363	Maserati	No	Car	Automobile	US
364	Massanfertigung-hemden.de	Yes	Shirt	Apparel	DE
365	massbett.de	Yes	Bed	Furniture	DE
366	masstisch.de	Yes	Table	Furniture	DE
367	MAXX	No	Bicycle	Sport & Leisure	DE
368	Mazda	No	Car	Automobile	DE
369	Mazda UK	No	Car	Automobile	UK
370	me and marta	Yes	Bag	Accessories	DE
371	Medical Electronics	No	Magnetic Field Therapy	Health	AT
372	mein-dirndl	Yes	Dirndl	Apparel	DE
373	MeineBackstube.de	No	Bread	Food	DE
374	Meine Kreation	Yes	Bag	Accessories	DE
375	Mein Kuscheltier Tagebuch	Yes	Personalized Book	Children's Products	FR
376	Mein-Notizbuch	Yes	Notebook	Stationery	DE
377	MeinSpiel	Yes	Playing Cards	Entertainment	DE
378	Mein Taschenkalender	Yes	Calendar	Print	DE
379	mein-wandkalender.de	Yes	Calendar	Print	DE
380	MEL BOTERI	Yes	Bag	Accessories	US
381	meMARMELADE	Yes	Marmalade	Food	DE
382	Memoir of me	Yes	Book	Print	US
383	MemorableGifts.com	Yes	Giftware	Giftware	US
384	Message on a Blanket	Yes	Baby Blanket	Children's Products	US
385	Micamisa	Yes	Shirt	Apparel	DE
386	milk & honey	Yes	Shoes	Footwear	US
387	Mini	No	Car	Automobile	DE
388	Misco	Yes	Computer	Electronics	DE
389	Mission Bicycle Company	Yes	Bicycle	Sport & Leisure	US
390	MIXA	Yes	USB Stick	Electronics	UK
391	Mixi Müsli	Yes	Cereal	Food	DE
392	Moen Incorporated	No	Kitchen	Construction	US
393	MojaMix	Yes	Cereal	Food	US
394	Mongoose Books	Yes	Book	Print	US
395	monofaktur	Yes	Design Foil	House & Garden	DE
396	Montech	No	Conveyor Belt	Industry	CH

	Company	Order Online?	Product	Industries	Country
397	Moormann	No	Storage Rack	Furniture	DE
398	morseketten	Yes	Morse Code Necklace	Accessories	DE
399	motivbriefkasten.de	Yes	Mailbox	House & Garden	DE
400	Mottega	Yes	Lamp	Furniture	US
401	Mueslimixer	Yes	Cereal	Food	US
402	Mulberry Moon	Yes	Soap	Beauty	US
403	Müller Maßmanufaktur	Yes	Shirt	Apparel	DE
404	MUNICH	Yes	Shoes	Footwear	ES
405	Murals Your Way	Yes	Murals	Print	US
406	Mutisun	Yes	Sun Lotion	Beauty	DE
407	MyBambino	Yes	Giftware	Giftware	US
408	MyBarong.com	Yes	Shirt	Apparel	US
409	MyBelt	Yes	Belt	Accessories	DE
410	mybesttable	No	Table	Furniture	DE
411	Mycasinocards.com	Yes	Playing Cards	Entertainment	US
412	My Choc	Yes	Chocolate	Food	DE
413	My Create-A-Book	Yes	Children's Book	Print	US
414	MyCustomTailor.com	Yes	Shirt	Apparel	TH
415	Mydallions	Yes	Golf Markers	Sport & Leisure	US
416	My Dogtag	Yes	Dog Tag	Accessories	CA
417	MyExtraGum	Yes	Gum	Food	US
418	myfotowall	Yes	Wallpaper	Print	UK
419	MyGall	Yes	Picture Frame	Giftware	DE
420	myJones	Yes	Label For Bottle	Giftware	US
421	MyKleenexTissue.com	Yes	Tissue Box	Giftware	US
422	mylavo	Yes	Clothes	Apparel	DE
423	mymat	Yes	Floor Mat	House & Garden	DE
424	MY M&M'S	Yes	Chocolate Candy	Food	US
425	My Monopoly Team	Yes	Monopoly Board	Entertainment	UK
426	mymuesli	Yes	Cereal	Food	DE
427	My Ordner	Yes	Folder	Print	DE
428	My Own Cookie	Yes	Fortune Cookie	Food	US
429	MyPacifier.com	Yes	Pacifier	Children's Products	US
430	MYPARFUEM	Yes	Perfume	Beauty	DE
431	My-Pebbles	Yes	Memory Stone	Giftware	DE
432	myprivatecode	Yes	Jewelry	Accessories	AT

	Company	Order Online?	Product	Industries	Country
433	mySN Schenker–Notebook	Yes	Computer	Electronics	DE
434	My Starbucks Signature	No	Drink	Food	US
435	myStofftier	Yes	Soft Toy	Children's Products	DE
437	mySwissChocolate	Yes	Chocolate	Food	CH
438	MyTailor.com	Yes	Shirt	Apparel	US
439	my twinn	Yes	Doll	Children's Products	US
440	My Unique Bag	Yes	Bag	Accessories	DE
441	My Virtual Model	No	Virtual Model	Service	US
442	Nagel	No	Garage	Construction	DE
443	nail-designer	Yes	Nails	Beauty	DE
444	Name Maker	Yes	Gift Wrap	Giftware	US
445	namensbaender	Yes	Custom Label	Advertising Material	DE
446	naturfaser-teppiche	Yes	Carpet	Furniture	DE
447	Neonsign.com	Yes	Neon Sign	Advertising Material	US
448	Netvibes	No	Custom Website	Media	UK
449	nflshop.com	Yes	T-Shirt	Apparel	US
450	Nike	Yes	Shoes	Footwear	US
451	Nilter	No	Custom Website	Media	DE
452	Nina Footwear	Yes	Shoes	Footwear	US
453	Nissan Deutschland	No	Car	Automobile	DE
454	North Shore Shirts	Yes	T-Shirt	Apparel	US
455	NovEx Hausbau	No	Prefabricated House	Construction	DE
456	Oakley	Yes	Sport Sunglasses	Optician	US
457	OBI@OTTO	Yes	Beach Chair	House & Garden	DE
458	Oelkrug Maßhemden	Yes	Shirt	Apparel	DE
459	Oetker Select	Yes	Cook Book	Print	DE
460	Offbeat Guides	Yes	Travel Guides	Sport & Leisure	US
461	Oh My Dog Supplies	Yes	Pet Bed	Equipment For Pets	US
462	Oliver Kahn	Yes	T-Shirt	Apparel	DE
463	Omega HTC	Yes	Pen	Stationery	US
464	O'Neill	No	Shoes	Footwear	US
465	OnTheBallBowling	Yes	Bowling Ball	Sport & Leisure	US
466	Optimalprint	Yes	Print Products	Print	NO
467	Original Home Plans	Yes	House Plans	Construction	US
468	ORISA	No	Hot Air Balloon	Sport & Leisure	DE
469	OrnamentShop.com	Yes	Christmas Ornament	Giftware	US

	Company	Order Online?	Product	Industries	Country
470	Paddock Way	Yes	Furniture	Furniture	US
471	Paintless Deco Impressions	Yes	T-Shirt	Apparel	US
472	palupas	Yes	Flip Flops	Footwear	DE
473	Party41.com	Yes	Party Equipment	Stationery	US
474	PartyBeans	Yes	Tin	Print	US
475	Partybox	Yes	Party Equipment	Stationery	US
476	Party Pong Tables	Yes	Beer Pong Table	Furniture	US
477	Party Sweets.com	Yes	Candy Wrapper	Print	US
478	Patria	No	Bicycle	Sport & Leisure	DE
479	PaulJulia Designs	Yes	Bag	Accessories	US
480	Paul Wolff	Yes	Garbage Can	Construction	DE
481	P.C. Peripherals	No	Computer	Electronics	IE
482	Pearlfection	Yes	Jewelry	Accessories	DE
483	Pelikan	No	Pen	Stationery	DE
484	Personal Headlines	Yes	Newspaper Headlines	Giftware	US
485	PersonalizationMall.com	Yes	Giftware	Giftware	US
486	Personalized Bike Plates.com	Yes	Bicycle Plates	Sport & Leisure	US
487	Personalized Boutique	Yes	Jewelry	Accessories	US
488	Personalized by Annette	Yes	Giftware	Giftware	US
489	Personalized Candy.com	Yes	Candy Bar Wrapper	Print	US
490	Personalized Creations	Yes	Giftware	Giftware	US
491	Personalized For Baby.com	Yes	Baby Equipment	Children's Products	US
492	Personalized Gifts.com	Yes	Bicycle Plates	Sport & Leisure	US
493	Personalizedgolfballs.com	Yes	Golf Equipment	Sport & Leisure	US
494	PersonalNOVEL	Yes	Book	Print	DE
495	Personello	Yes	Giftware	Giftware	DE
496	Pervino	Yes	Wine Label	Print	US
497	PetCollection	Yes	Watch	Accessories	US
498	Petra Diegel	No	Bag	Accessories	DE
499	Peugeot Austria	No	Car	Automobile	AT
500	Peugeot Deutschland	No	Car	Automobile	DE
501	Pflanzmich	Yes	Garden Plant	House & Garden	DE
502	PHD	Yes	Sleeping Bag	Sport & Leisure	US
503	Photolini	Yes	Photo Wall	Print	DE
504	PhotoShowerCurtain.com	Yes	Shower Curtain	House & Garden	US
505	PIACEMOLTO	Yes	Shirt	Apparel	IT

	Company	Order Online?	Product	Industries	Country
506	picasso head	No	Picture	Entertainment	US
507	Pickfactory	Yes	Guitar Picks	Giftware	NO
508	Picture Paper	Yes	Gift Wrap	Giftware	US
509	Pik7.de	Yes	Playing Cards	Entertainment	DE
510	PixelTalents	Yes	Canvas	Giftware	DE
511	Pixeltees	Yes	T-Shirt	Apparel	US
512	Pixie and the Prince	Yes	Baby Equipment	Children's Products	US
513	PlateCreator	Yes	Car Plates	Sport & Leisure	IE
514	pluddel	Yes	Gift Paper	Giftware	DE
515	PokaMax	Yes	Post Card	Giftware	DE
516	Ponoko	Yes	Art	Giftware	NZ
517	Poobies	Yes	Greeting Card	Stationery	US
518	Porsche Austria	No	Car	Automobile	AT
519	Post	Yes	Stamp	Giftware	AT
520	Postalo	Yes	Print Products	Print	DE
521	Preschoolians	Yes	Shoes	Footwear	US
522	Pretty Baby Gifts	Yes	Baby Gifts	Children's Products	US
523	PrinceHenry.biz	Yes	Clothes	Apparel	TH
524	Printakid	Yes	Book	Print	US
525	PrintPlanet	Yes	Giftware	Giftware	DE
526	printshirt24.de	Yes	T-Shirt	Apparel	DE
527	Proper Cloth	Yes	Shirt	Apparel	US
528	proTECH	No	Computer	Electronics	AT
529	Puget Systems	Yes	Computer	Electronics	US
530	PulpStar	Yes	Book	Print	US
531	PUMA	Yes	Shoes	Footwear	CH
532	Pursenal	Yes	Bag	Accessories	DE
533	Q'uchu	No	Cap	Accessories	DE
534	Ragaller	No	Food Package	Print	DE
535	Ralph Lauren	Yes	Shirt	Apparel	US
536	RavisTailor.com	Yes	Shirt	Apparel	US
537	Re-Bath	No	Bathroom	Construction	US
538	RedMoon Custom Pet Food	Yes	Pet Food	Equipment For Pets	US
539	Reebok	Yes	Shoes	Footwear	NL
540	REEDS Jewelers	Yes	Jewelry	Accessories	US
541	Regalsystem-max	No	Storage Rack	Furniture	DE

	Company	Order Online?	Product	Industries	Country
542	Regnauer Hausbau	No	Prefabricated House	Construction	DE
543	R.E.Load Baggage	Yes	Bag	Accessories	US
544	Renault Deutschland	No	Car	Automobile	DE
545	renesim	Yes	Jewelry	Accessories	DE
546	Renodom	No	Bathroom	Construction	DE
547	Republic Bike	Yes	Bicycle	Sport & Leisure	US
548	RestaurantBags.com	Yes	Restaurant Bag	Print	US
549	reva Werbeartikel	Yes	Polo Shirt	Apparel	AT
550	Revolution Snowboard Manufacturing	Yes	Snowboard	Sport & Leisure	US
551	RHO design	Yes	T-Shirt	Apparel	DE
552	Rich Company	Yes	Watch	Accessories	US
553	Rickshaw	Yes	Bag	Accessories	US
554	Rittal	Yes	Custom Enclosures	Electronics	DE
555	Rivolta	Yes	Shoes	Footwear	IT
556	Rockberries	Yes	Jewelry	Accessories	DE
557	Rohrbacher	No	Watch	Accessories	DE
558	Rooms By You	Yes	Rooms	House & Garden	US
559	Rose	Yes	Bicycle	Sport & Leisure	DE
560	ROTERFADEN	Yes	Bag	Accessories	DE
561	route one solutions	Yes	Clothes	Apparel	UK
562	Ruby	Yes	Helmet	Sport & Leisure	US
563	Ruby Fox	Yes	Bridal Lingerie	Apparel	US
564	Rug Couture	Yes	Rug	Furniture	UK
565	Running Banana	Yes	T-Shirt	Apparel	US
566	Ruukki	No	Facade Claddings	Steel	FI
567	Saab Deutschland	No	Car	Automobile	SE
568	Safari Sun	Yes	T-Shirt	Apparel	US
569	Saint Sens	Yes	Shirt	Apparel	FR
570	Samurai Swords Shop	Yes	Sword	Sport & Leisure	BE
571	Sandi's T's	Yes	T-Shirt	Apparel	US
572	Sara's Shoes	Yes	Shoes	Footwear	US
573	Saxoprint	Yes	Office Equipment	Stationery	DE
574	scake	Yes	Cake	Print	DE
575	Scarfmaker	Yes	Scarf	Apparel	US
576	Schatzinsel Schmuck	Yes	Necklace	Giftware	DE

	Company	Order Online?	Product	Industries	Country
577	Schlotterer	No	Roller Blind	House & Garden	DE
578	Schnuller mit Namen	Yes	Pacifier	Children's Products	DK
579	schornstein markt	Yes	Chimney	Construction	DE
580	Sculpteo	Yes	Figure	Entertainment	FR
581	Searchbots	No	Search Engine Help	Service	US
582	SEAT Deutschland	No	Car	Automobile	DE
583	Segway	No	Personal Transporter	Transportation	UK
584	SEIZ	Yes	Backpack	Sport & Leisure	ES
585	s.e.l.v.e.	Yes	Shoes	Footwear	DE
586	Sendgiftbaskets	Yes	Gift Basket	Giftware	US
587	Set26	No	Storage Rack	Furniture	CH
588	Seton	Yes	Parking Signs	Advertising Material	US
589	Shapeways	Yes	Art	Giftware	NL
590	shirt30.de	Yes	T-Shirt	Apparel	DE
591	shirtalarm	Yes	T-Shirt	Apparel	DE
592	ShirtArt	Yes	T-Shirt	Apparel	DE
593	shirtbuster	Yes	T-Shirt	Apparel	DE
594	ShirtbyHand	Yes	Shirt	Apparel	NL
595	SHIRTCITY	Yes	T-Shirt	Apparel	DE
596	Shirtcreations	Yes	Shirt	Apparel	US
597	Shirtfather.eu	Yes	T-Shirt	Apparel	DE
598	Shirtfriends AG	Yes	T-Shirt	Apparel	DE
599	shirtin	No	T-Shirt	Apparel	DE
600	Shirtinator AG	Yes	T-Shirt	Apparel	DE
601	ShirtMagic	Yes	T-Shirt	Apparel	US
602	Shirtman.de	Yes	T-Shirt	Apparel	DE
603	ShirtPainter.com	Yes	T-Shirt	Apparel	DE
604	Shirtracer	Yes	T-Shirt	Apparel	DE
605	shirtsbedrucken.de	Yes	T-Shirt	Apparel	DE
606	ShirtsMyWay	Yes	Shirt	Apparel	US
607	Shirts-Selbst-Bedrucken.de	Yes	T-Shirt	Apparel	DE
608	Shirt-x	Yes	T-Shirt	Apparel	DE
609	Shoes of Prey	Yes	Shoes	Footwear	AU
610	Shortomatic.com	Yes	Shorts	Apparel	US
611	SIMPLON	No	Bicycle	Sport & Leisure	AT
612	simply colors	Yes	Baby Clothes	Apparel	DE

	Company	Order Online?	Product	Industries	Country
613	Simply Scrumptous	Yes	Cookie	Food	US
614	SJC Drums	Yes	Drum Kit	Music	US
615	Skinit	Yes	Skin	Electronics	US
616	Skoda	No	Car	Automobile	DE
617	Slant Shack Jerky	Yes	Meat	Food	US
618	smart	No	Car	Automobile	US
619	Smart Furniture	Yes	Storage Rack	Furniture	US
620	smarthaus	No	House Color System	Construction	DE
621	Smart Jeans	Yes	Jeans	Apparel	AT
622	Smart Shirt	Yes	Shirt	Apparel	CN
623	SnackSelect	Yes	Snacks	Food	DE
624	Snapfish	Yes	Giftware	Giftware	US
625	Snaptotes	Yes	Bag	Accessories	US
626	Sneakart	Yes	Shoes	Footwear	UK
627	Sockprints	Yes	Socks	Apparel	US
628	Soft Star Shoes	Yes	Soft Shoes	Footwear	US
629	Software Partner	Yes	USB Stick	Electronics	DE
630	Solosso	Yes	Shirt	Apparel	CH
631	Sonnenkorb	No	Beach Chair	House & Garden	AT
632	Sonnenkorb.ch	No	Beach Chair	House & Garden	CH
633	Sonnenschutz24	Yes	Roller Blind	House & Garden	DE
634	Sonntagmorgen Kaffee	Yes	Coffee	Food	DE
635	specialtyribbon	Yes	Custom Ribbon	Giftware	US
636	SpeedySigns	Yes	Banner	Advertising Material	US
637	Spoleto	No	Food	Food	ES
638	Spoonflower	Yes	Fabrics	Apparel	US
639	spreadshirt	Yes	T-Shirt	Apparel	DE
640	Spreewald-praesente.de	Yes	Gift Basket	Food	DE
641	SQ2 Drum System	No	Drums	Music	DE
642	STABILO	No	Pen	Stationery	DE
643	Stamps.com	Yes	Photo Stamps	Stationery	US
644	Stein Diamonds	Yes	Ring	Accessories	US
645	Stevens Bikes	Yes	Bicycle	Sport & Leisure	DE
646	Stickiestory	Yes	Book	Print	AR
647	stoff'n	Yes	Fabrics	Apparel	DE
648	Stoff-Reich	Yes	Dirndl	Apparel	DE
649	Stoffschmiede	Yes	Fabrics	Apparel	DE

	Company	Order Online?	Product	Industries	Country
650	Storytime Personalized Books	Yes	Children's Book	Print	US
651	Stratec Medizintechnik	No	Medical Technology	Electronics	DE
652	streetshirts	Yes	T-Shirt	Apparel	UK
653	STREIF	No	Cladding Color	Construction	DE
654	Studio Ludens	Yes	Coaster	House & Garden	NL
655	style-ich	Yes	Giftware	Giftware	DE
656	Subway	No	Sandwiches	Food	US
657	sumosam	Yes	T-Shirt	Apparel	UK
658	Sunclipies	Yes	Glasses	Accessories	US
659	superstructs	Yes	Kit Toys	Giftware	US
660	Surfboardbuilders.com	Yes	Surfboard	Sport & Leisure	US
661	Suzuki Swift	No	Car	Automobile	AT
662	SwimCapz	Yes	Swim Caps	Sport & Leisure	CA
663	Taaz.com	Yes	Virtual Makeup	Beauty	US
664	tailor4less	Yes	Suit	Apparel	CH
665	Tailorcut.com	Yes	Shirt	Apparel	CH
666	Tailored Shirts	Yes	Shirt	Apparel	HK
667	Tailor Store	Yes	Shirt	Apparel	CH
668	Tailory	Yes	Shirt	Apparel	DE
669	TakeOutTees.com	Yes	Clothes	Apparel	US
670	Tanner+Tailor	Yes	Bag	Accessories	DE
671	TasteBook	Yes	Book	Giftware	US
672	Teckentrup	No	Garage Door	Construction	DE
673	Teeki Hut	Yes	T-Shirt	Apparel	US
674	TeeshirtsDirect.com	Yes	T-Shirt	Apparel	UK
675	Terrific-Tubes	Yes	Lamp	Furniture	DE
676	TETZNER & JENTZISCH	No	Fence	Construction	DE
677	That's My Pan!	Yes	Giftware	Giftware	US
678	The Cereal Club	Yes	Cereal	Food	DE
679	The Crown Royal Company	Yes	Bag	Giftware	US
680	The EC Store	Yes	Underwear	Apparel	US
681	The Elegant Child	Yes	Baby Equipment	Children's Products	US
682	The Eton T-Shirt Co.	Yes	T-Shirt	Apparel	UK
683	TheFedoraStore.com	Yes	Hat	Accessories	US
684	The Left Shoe Company	Yes	Shoes	Footwear	FI
685	The McGraw-Hill Companies	Yes	Book	Print	US

	Company	Order Online?	Product	Industries	Country
686	The Reef Screen Builder	No	Digital Poster	Entertainment	US
687	The Sak	No	Bag	Accessories	US
688	THE SCENT OF ART	Yes	Shoes	Footwear	US
689	The Shirt Printer.com	Yes	T-Shirt	Apparel	US
690	The Stationery Studio	Yes	Giftware	Giftware	US
691	The Teehive	Yes	T-Shirt	Apparel	US
692	Thomas Möller Werbemittel	Yes	Chrome Letters	Automobile	DE
693	ThyssenKrupp	No	Elevator	Construction	DE
694	ThyssenKrupp Aufzüge	No	Elevator	Steel	AT
695	Timberland Company	Yes	Shoes	Footwear	US
696	Timbuk2	Yes	Bag	Accessories	US
697	Time and Date.com	No	Calendar	Stationery	NO
698	timissimo	Yes	Watch	Accessories	DE
699	Tiny Pocket People	Yes	Pocket Doll	Children's Products	SE
700	TOPIC	No	Door	Construction	AT
701	Toyota Deutschland	No	Car	Automobile	DE
702	Transtec	Yes	Computer	Electronics	AT
703	Trashic.ch	Yes	Shirt	Apparel	CH
704	Trek Bicycle Corporation	No	Bicycle	Sport & Leisure	US
705	Trendgifts Gerhard Hess	Yes	Baby Bottle	Children's Products	DE
706	Trikotex	No	Jersey	Apparel	DE
707	TRUE	Yes	Jacket	Apparel	NZ
708	truttigtegeltje.eu	Yes	Tile	Print	NL
709	t-shirt-druck.com	Yes	T-Shirt	Apparel	DE
710	TShirt-Druck-X	Yes	Clothes	Apparel	DE
711	T-Shirts.com	Yes	T-Shirt	Apparel	US
712	TShirt Studio	Yes	T-Shirt	Apparel	UK
713	T-Shirt-Total.de	Yes	T-Shirt	Apparel	DE
714	Tweetnotebook.com	Yes	Book	Print	BE
715	UberPrints.com	Yes	T-Shirt	Apparel	US
716	Ujeans	No	Jeans	Apparel	US
717	Uncommon	Yes	Mobile Phone Cover	Electronics	US
718	Unser Geschenkbuch	Yes	Book	Giftware	DE
719	UO Bike Shop	Yes	Bicycle	Sport & Leisure	US
720	Upper Street London	Yes	Shoes	Footwear	UK
721	Uupsis	Yes	Soft Toy	Children's Products	DE

	Company	Order Online?	Product	Industries	Country
722	Valentins	Yes	Beer Label	Giftware	DE
723	Van Nicholas	No	Bicycle	Sport & Leisure	US
724	Vans	Yes	Shoes	Footwear	US
725	varistyle	No	Hangings	Furniture	DE
726	Vaust	Yes	Bicycle	Sport & Leisure	DE
727	Very Cool T-shirts	Yes	T-Shirt	Apparel	US
728	Vicale Corporation	Yes	Action Figure	Children's Products	US
729	VictoryStore.com	Yes	Shirt	Apparel	US
730	Videomedia	Yes	Video	Entertainment	DE
731	Viesso	Yes	Furniture	Furniture	US
732	VIRTUALSHIRT	Yes	T-Shirt	Apparel	DE
733	VisionBedding	Yes	Bedding	House & Garden	US
734	Vistaprint	Yes	Office Equipment	Stationery	FR
735	VOLKSWAGEN AG	No	Car	Automobile	DE
736	Volvo Car Germany	Yes	Car	Automobile	DE
737	VW of America	No	Car	Automobile	US
738	Wackymats.com	Yes	Floor Mat	House & Garden	US
739	WADOO	Yes	Giftware	Giftware	DE
740	Walmart	Yes	Ring	Accessories	US
741	WANDWORTE	Yes	Wall Tattoo	Print	DE
742	Waterland House	Yes	T-Shirt	Apparel	UK
743	WE	Yes	Shirt	Apparel	NL
744	WearYourCity.com	Yes	T-Shirt	Apparel	US
745	wechselwild.com	Yes	Belt	Accessories	DE
746	Wedding Paper Divas	Yes	Wedding Stationery	Stationery	US
747	WeLoveFruits	Yes	Snacks	Food	DE
748	Werbebanner24	Yes	Advertising Ad	Advertising Material	DE
749	WERMA Signaltechnik	No	Signal Pillar	Electronics	DE
750	WhiteSalmonBoatWorks.com	Yes	Boat	Sport & Leisure	US
751	Whoopass Enterprises	Yes	Body Doll	Entertainment	US
752	Wildemasche	Yes	Scarf	Apparel	DE
753	Wine Label	Yes	Wine Label	Print	US
754	Winkhaus	No	Access Control	Construction	DE
755	WOONIO	Yes	Furniture	Furniture	DE
756	Wrench Science	Yes	Bicycle	Sport & Leisure	US
757	Wristbands with a Message.com	Yes	Wristband	Accessories	US

	Company	Order Online?	Product	Industries	Country
758	Wunschcurry	Yes	Spices	Food	DE
759	Wunschfutter	Yes	Pet Food	Equipment For Pets	DE
760	WunschKeks.de	Yes	Fortune Cookies	Giftware	DE
761	Wunschlikör	Yes	Liqueur	Giftware	DE
762	WUWI	Yes	T-Shirt	Apparel	UK
763	Xada	Yes	Computer	Electronics	DE
764	Yearmadeforme	Yes	Planner	Stationery	US
765	yellochip.de	Yes	Computer	Electronics	DE
766	YIT Corporation	No	Kitchen Color Design	Construction	FI
767	yogamatic.com	Yes	Yoga Mat	Sport & Leisure	US
768	YouBar	Yes	Nutrition Bar	Food	US
769	You design it	Yes	T-Shirt	Apparel	US
770	youniik	Yes	Skins	Electronics	DE
771	Your Bookshelf	Yes	Shelf	Furniture	DE
772	your-design	Yes	Wall Tattoo	Print	DE
773	Your Design	Yes	Giftware	Giftware	US
774	Your M&S	Yes	Shirt	Apparel	UK
775	yournovel.com	Yes	Book	Print	US
776	Yourplayingcards.com	Yes	Playing Cards	Entertainment	US
777	YourSurprise.com	Yes	Giftware	Giftware	NL
778	yourwovenphotos.com	Yes	Music Box	Music	US
779	You Tailor	Yes	Suit	Apparel	AT
780	Zales Jewelers	Yes	Ring	Accessories	US
781	Zazzle Inc.	Yes	Giftware	Giftware	US
782	zick shirt.de	Yes	T-Shirt	Apparel	DE
783	Zipline Golf	Yes	Golf Ball	Sport & Leisure	US

Country Abbreviation	Country Name
AR	Argentina
AT	Austria
AU	Australia
BE	Belgium
CA	Canada
CH	Switzerland
CN	China, People's Republic of
CZ	Czech Republic
DE	Germany
DK	Denmark
ES	Spain
FI	Finland
FR	France
HK	China, Hong Kong
IE	Ireland
IN	India
IT	Italy
LT	Lithuania
NL	Netherlands
NO	Norway
NZ	New Zealand
SE	Sweden
TH	Thailand
UK	United Kingdom
US	United States

Index

L

M